With the rise of domestic vi
Do No Harm by Richard Villasana is an important book for any-one who wants to help children in crisis. Villasana shines the light of awareness on an issue that society needs to confront. I am grateful for this book and recommend it to all who wish to make a difference in our world.

—Dr. John DeGarmo, Leading Foster Care Expert
Founder/Director of The Foster Care Institute

There are few people in this country more dedicated to finding family members in Latin America for kids who find themselves lost or alone at our border more than Richard Villasana. "Do No Harm" is sure to be a mainstay for those involved in the field. He lends his experience and knowledge of the subject garnered by his countless amount of time on the front line. This book will benefit generations of people working toward solutions.

—Chris Chmielewski Editor, Foster Focus magazine

There is what people want us to believe and what is really hap-pening. This is a must-read book for anyone concerned about our children and what is being done to help them. Thank you, Richard, for this wonderful insight and for the many of countless hours you put into getting familiar reunited with their children.

—Daniel Gutierrez
-International Best-Selling Author, Speaker, Mindful Leadership Expert, Master Life/Business Coach, Director/ Owner of Catalina Retreat Center in San Salvador, Peru

Richard Villasana and his book, "Do No Harm – An American Tragedy Continues" is an extremely important book for anyone who actually cares about children. What is described in this book is not just a national crisis – it is an International crisis, and how this crisis has been allowed to continue is appalling. What happened to the American dream of economic opportunity and freedom? There are definitive actions that government agencies, politicians, and each one of us can take to make positive changes in foster care. It's time we focus on solutions. How many more children must be abused and/or killed before we find a solution? As citizens of our country, we each have a role to play in making a better world for our children. This book will pave the way for those changes.

—Tom Antion
https://www.GreatInternetMarketingTraining.com

An American Tragedy indeed. The impact of the injustice and pain experienced by these children and their families is heart-wrenching. Children are the future, and this tragedy will have an impact long after most of us are gone from this earth. Richard Villasana is a maverick leader whose sole mission comes from the depth of his soul. As he so eloquently shares, we are an intelligent society of human beings. We can unite to solve this issue. There is no keener revelation of a society's health and wealth than how it treats its children.

—Steve Olsher
Founder/Editor-In-Chief of Podcast Magazine
& NYT Bestselling Author of What Is Your WHAT?
Discover The ONE Amazing Thing You Were Born To Do

This book, Do No Harm, An American Tragedy Continues is a must-read for understanding the true story of what's going on in immigration and foster care. Read this eye-opening book and take in the full scope of what is happening to innocent children. Let's find a solution for this tragedy!

—Jill Lublin 4x bestselling author,
master publicity strategist and international speaker
http://PublicityCrashCourse.com

In Do No Harm by Richard Villasana, the founder of Forever Homes for Foster Kids, Richard brings to light the challenges that face foster children. Being a Real Estate investor, realizing that the future for these children is homelessness and poverty, I am determined to create additional creative partnership opportunities that allow more families to get ahead in life. Thanks, Richard for bringing this harsh reality to our attention where we can make strides to move forward towards making a difference in these foster kids' futures.

—Peter Vekselman
Real Estate Trainer and Coach, PartnerDriven.com

As a former CASA advocate, I've witnessed firsthand the enormous flaws in the foster care system caused by an interlaced network of external issues. Raising seven children of my own, my heart breaks for the thousands of children seemingly lost in the foster care system, through no fault of their own.

This book, Do No Harm, An American Tragedy Continues, details explicitly the stark reality that billions of dollars are poured into a system, which fails 80% of the time.

Richard Villasana details his experience on the front-line while tasked with locating some of the worst cold cases of children lost in the foster care system.

Do No Harm is indeed a riveting book and precisely the shock-value needed to send a urgent message to those directly responsible for implementing effective positive change, in a tragically flawed-system. A system originally designed to protect and nurture the most vulnerable—the children.

—Dana L. Banks
Former CASA advocate, Public Speaker and Author

Richard's new book, Do No Harm, shines the light of presence on an area of our society that has grown darker as the masses continue to turn their backs on the silent epidemic that has gained even more momentum in recent years. This is not a foster care problem. This is "our" problem now. This book is a must-read. Every child needs love and a guiding presence in their life to have a chance. I trust this book will reach a wide enough audience to bring the problem to full awareness. Only then will there be a chance for a better way. This book details many young people's tragedies, sorrow, and loss of hope. This book can be a catalyst to change the future of so many if embraced.

—Austin Haines
Motivational Speaker, Flashpoint Documentarian &
Power of Pure Presence TV Show Host

Do No Harm by Richard Villasana is a gripping read that's sure to increase your awareness on the tragic reality of what happens to so many kids in the foster care system. Someone needs to tell this story from the raw realities of what most of us don't see. Richard nails this as he really dives deep with full transparency on a subject we should all pay closer attention to. What a powerful book!

—Jose Escobar
CEO & Founder of The Entrepreneur's Bookshelf

In my world travels to 103 countries, I've observed children of all ethnicities living a life of poverty and distress, orphaned like those mentioned in Richard Villasans's book, "Do No Harm." Therefore, as cofounder of TheKeepSmilingMovement. org, I consider it part of my legacy to support organizations like Forever Homes for Foster Kids to give kids a dose of hope through smiles. Honored to know you, Richard.

—Ken "Dr. Smiley" Rochon, Jr.
Cofounder, TheKeepSmilingMovement.org;
Celebrity Event Photographer, The Umbrella Syndicate;
Publisher, PerfectPublishing.com

Witnessing severe traumatizing lifelong challenges for foster care children from infancy to adulthood brings this reality to the forefront. As a former 911 emergency dispatcher, corrections officer, CASA/GAL advocate, and a former adjunct college professor teaching law enforcement classes including sexually violent crime investigation, knowing Richard Villasana's "Forever

Homes for Foster Kids" exists provides solace. They advocate for the health, safety, and permanent placement of innocent kids. Embracing possibility, we come together as a community to give kids hope, a smile, and a forever home.

—Dr. Andrea Adams-Miller, **CEO**
http://TheREDCarpetConnection.com
International Publicity Agency; Executive Director of Happiness,
http://TheKeepSmilingMovement.org,

Mental and Dental Health Advocacy; and Board Member,
http://YouAreMyLightFoundation.org
(YAML) Human Trafficking Advocacy

We have all heard tales of the dilemma happening at the Southern border of our country. Yet, few of us truly understand what is happening. Families seeking asylum as they cross the border into our country are apprehended, imprisoned, separated from their children, and then deported back to their countries. Many children are placed in a broken foster care system – often never reunited with their families. But Richard Villasana is working tirelessly to educate and remedy the situation. For anyone who believes in the humanity in all of us, this book is a must-read!

—Ellen Violette
Books Open Doors® Coaching & Author Services - Named Top 20 Book Coach of 2022 by CoachFoundation
https://booksopendoors.com

As I read Richard Villasana's book, I was struck by these powerful words: *"The future for most of these kids is becoming homeless, turning to crime so they have enough money for food and shelter, becoming a sex trafficking victim – sometimes in a little as six hours – or ending up in prison or dead within a year of aging out."* The magnitude of this and the responsibility of society to stem this tide is paramount. Richard's book is truly a wake-up call and truly sobering. The book is a testament to the truth people don't want to talk about. Highly recommend it.

Richard Villasana in the book Do No Harm, does a dynamic job giving a much-needed amplified voice of the children that have either been silenced or terrorized into compliance and submission by a system designed to help them. This particular sub-group of children are even more vulnerable to falling between the cracks of our social-justice system and this book captures the raw, unaltered, essence of their stories with eye-opening touches of the resilience of the human spirit. As an adult who was a young child forced to navigate the cruel, emotionless machine of the foster care system- I can without a doubt attest to the validity of the reality that is described in this book. This book is a must read. We all have a responsibility to protect the most venerable members of our society and this book is the prefect catalyst to start the necessary open-dialog to transform how people approach this issue.

—Mel EB

Richard Villasana, a bi-national guardian angel who works to spare children the pain of family separation.

—Ruben Navarrette Jr.
https://www.ukiahdailyjournal.com/2019/01/08/
from-the-desk-of-a-guardian-angel-on-the-border-
comes-to-the-rescue/

A book that's an endorsement of change and NOT an indictment of the status quo. "Do No Harm" is as refreshing as it is enlightening. I fell in love with the stories, the successes, and the failures. The kids who found and re-found loving, permanent, homes and those who didn't. There's no judgement here, just the observable phenomena that kids are dying for us to solve the puzzle of the foster care system, for Latinos, and us all.

—Jackie Simmons
Creator of Conscious Transformational Coaching
Co-founder and Director of the
Teen Suicide Prevention Society

Not only does Richard Villasana expose what is happening to the children of our world – particularly within our own country – but he also offers viable and workable solutions. Pick up a copy of this book, read it. Pay close attention to chapter fourteen – Fixing Foster Care for All Children. Then find it on your heart to tap into the suggestions he gave that will make a difference.

—Gia Heller
CEO of the Social Media Masters

DO NO HARM

DO NO HARM

An American Tragedy Continues

BY
RICHARD VILLASANA
Founder of Forever Homes for Foster Kids

Spotlight PUBLISHING
Goodyear, AZ

Table of Contents

Dedication

This book is dedicated to the three powerful, amazing women who are in my life: Cristina Villasana, my love; my mother, Ana J. Villasana, who has been my rock; and Libbe HaLevy, writer and editor as well as one of my dearest friends and compadre.

This book is also dedicated to the thousands of parents who came to the U.S. hoping to give their children a better, safer life. Theirs is the sacrifice of true love for their child.

Acknowledgements

Nobody writes a book in isolation if you want to put out a book worth reading. This is my opportunity to thank those who have supported and inspired me. This book would not have been possible if I had not met my mentor, Antoine Morrison. He spent years teaching me about international business and the importance of culture and history to excel in Latin America. He also taught me many life lessons. I hope I've done him proud.

I want to thank my mastermind partners, Libbe HaLevy, producer/host of the internationally awarded podcast Nuclear Hotseat, and Donald Hunter, CEO of GreaterUp, a leadership development company. Both have motivated and pushed me along to focus and write this book. My appreciation to Jill Lublin, my publicity mentor. She's the reason my message has been televised in the U.S. and throughout Latin America. A special thank you to my great friends: Mike and Chela Davis, who have supported me and my work with their encouragement and generosity and Dwight and Claudia Fowler who have been with me through the worst of times and the best.

Of course, this book would not have been written without the help of Christopher Mele of bettergetaneditor.com who provided the structure and flow of the book.

I appreciate my mom, Ana J. Villasana, for her editorial encouragement and sharp eye. Thanks to Beth Terry, my administrative assistant, who took a lot of work off my shoulders.

A huge thank you to our team members in Latin America who have worked so diligently to locate relatives for immigrant and U.S. foster children: Paula Muñoz, Monica Contreras, Marvin Delcid, Valery Figueroa, Aida Flores and Gabriela Castaneda.

Finally, thank you to our Brazil and Caribbean specialist, Natali Souza.

I appreciate all of you for being in my life and helping me to grow as I chase after my vision: For each foster child to have a permanent home.

Introduction

More than 423,900 children are in U.S. foster care.

Today 55 kids will disappear from their foster homes. Most will never be found.

Roughly 66 foster teens will age out and be forced into the streets and on their own tonight.

By tomorrow morning, some of the foster teens who age out today will be sex trafficking victims, essentially slaves.

Welcome to the United States foster care system.

Child experts, caseworkers and judges are generally in agreement that foster care is not the best place for a child to spend years of their young lives. The system was never intended to be a government institution that raises children until adulthood. Too often children who do remain in foster care suffer a lack of stability with constant moves from one home to another, frustration with losing friends and adults who care about them and long-term depression.

Nearly 23,000 foster teens are forced out (usually called "aging out") of the system annually, and their lifetime statistics are appalling and obscene.

- Between 20-30 percent will become homeless, some immediately.
- Upwards of 40 percent must find ways to complete their high school education while searching for food and safe shelter.
- Some foster teens become sex trafficking victims in as little as six hours.
- Thousands end up in prison.
- Some will be killed or commit suicide.

These terrible outcomes usually occur within just two years of foster kids being forced out of the system. If these statistics aren't enough to grab your attention, then let's put some dollars to this problem.

Michael Reagan, son of President Ronald Reagan, in his article, "Foster Kids Need Support Past 18," wrote, *"Foster children who age out cost the state an average of $300,000 in social costs over the former foster child's lifetime."* It is estimated that foster children who will age out of the system this year will cost taxpayers $7.2 billion. The kids aging out next year will cost taxpayers another $7.2 billion. Houston, Texas is reported to have roughly 200 children forced out of foster care each year, so its costs will be about $60 million, or the equivalent of having 223 teenagers housed and educated at Harvard University for four years.

Why would you care? Part of that $7.2 billion is your tax dollars. Does it sound like you are getting your money's worth? Doesn't sound like it to me.

Nearly 30 percent of foster teens will never get a high school diploma because they are subject to frequent moves, and each school district has its own guidelines as to what classes will be accepted. The foster care system cannot guarantee smooth sailing. It cannot guarantee long-term stability or even a good environment for the children placed under its care.

Do you think a child should be in an environment where many are getting slapped, beaten, starved, molested and killed? Didn't think so. You are a good-hearted person who would rather know your tax dollars and government are working hard to ensure that each child in foster care gets a chance at a much better future with a permanent, forever family. Best of all, most of this pain and suffering by children is preventable, not in five or ten years, but NOW.

Fortunately, there is a solution. Family finding can prevent these horrific outcomes. What is family finding? It is a process of identifying, locating and notifying relatives who can and want to provide love, support and protection for a child from their own family. Even if the child is a teenager, at least they will have a chance to connect with their relatives who can help the teen better transition into adulthood. Barring reunification with a parent or other family members, the results of an intense and experienced family finding process can open the door for an adoption to move forward, making this effort a vitally important process.

The family finding concept is simple – find and notify enough relatives and someone, a grandmother, aunt, uncle or adult cousin, will step up and take in the child. Family finding is one of the simplest and most effective procedures in foster care to get children out of the system. If this isn't at least tried, children who could be placed with family end up spending years, if not their entire childhood, in foster care and age out with no family connections.

Unfortunately, family finding is suffering a quiet and ignored crisis. The white paper, "What is Family Finding and Engagement?" by the California Social Work Education Center (CalSWEC) states that several advocates, including the Children's Defense Fund, define family finding as:

> *"The practice of rigorously searching for and engaging extended family members and other supportive adults to establish an enduring support network for children."*

> *"Intensive relative search and engagement techniques to identify family and other close adults for children in foster care."*

> *"An intensive search method to find family members."*

The operative words in these definitions are "intensive" and "rigorous." To apply these terms, there must be some standardization of the family finding process. Only then can we check the baseline, meaning where we are presently in relation to the outcome we want to achieve.

While many foster care agencies across the country have formal procedures in place, there is little oversight to ensure that each agency's family finding is intensive. Too many offices treat family finding as an optional activity while some agencies don't even have a formal family finding structure.

Now let's look at doing family finding internationally because there are more than 91,000 Latino children in U.S. foster care today. For the majority we're talking about children who are U.S. citizens with at least one U.S.-born parent. Searching for and finding a person in another country takes additional expertise beyond looking for someone who lives in the U.S. Virtually no university in the United States specifically teaches about family finding. Many government foster care agencies do not provide training.

Caseworkers are not likely to develop this expertise unless they receive appropriate training, but that is certainly not being given today. It's a fact that some social workers are overburdened with 40 to 70 foster child cases. In the AP article, "Judge: Texas is to blame for foster care neglect, failures," U.S. District Judge Janis Graham Jack gave a scathing rebuke of the Texas Department of Family and Protective Services because:

> *"more and more of them [foster kids] were looked after by case workers whose training amounted to as little as a 60-minute video on how to care for troubled kids."*

One of the most critically important functions of caseworkers is to care for troubled kids who have been traumatized and abused. Now just imagine the insanity of expecting these same caseworkers who are not receiving quality trauma training to somehow receive any kind of training that will prepare them to successfully locate a foster child's family members in a Latin American country.

As an expert in international marketing in Latin America, I can tell you that there is a significant difference from doing business in the U.S. and doing business in another country. Dealing successfully with another country involves different skill sets, expertise and ongoing training. Consequently, the reality is that there is simply no time or training for virtually any caseworker to develop a level of expertise where they can consistently do successful family finding in another country.

Sadly, the result for thousands of Latino foster children is that family finding is performed by untrained social workers where the results fall far short of the legal federal mandate that:

> *"within 30 days after the removal of a child from the custody of the parent or parents of the child, the State shall exercise due diligence to identify and provide notice to all adult grandparents and other adult relatives of the child (including any other adult relatives suggested by the parents)."*

Poor family finding means that tens of thousands of Latino foster children are left in the system for years, many until they age out. Those who are forced out of foster care at age 18 or 21 leave with no family connections or support.

This crisis of failing to reunite thousands of Latino foster children with their relatives is about to have a meltdown because thousands of immigrant children, many now unaccompanied by any adult, have been and are passing through the federal system and ending up in foster care.

Throughout the last two years several thousands of parents, caregivers and foster parents have become disabled or died. Counties across the U.S. are pleading with people to become foster parents. Just as we are hearing across the U.S. and the world about critically ill people being turned away because of the lack of hospital beds, doctors and nurses, a wave of immigrant children could easily push the foster care system, already in crisis, into such a damaged state that it may take years or even decades to recover.

But at the end of the day, it's not the foster care system that deserves our attention and sympathy. It's the thousands of Latino children, immigrant and U.S.-born, who are suffering. It is children being placed in a system that instead of protecting them often abuses and, for some, kills them.

Many do not or will never receive the proper care to address their trauma, depression and, for some, suicidal thoughts. It's lonely, scared, isolated Latino children who most likely will suffer years in the U.S. foster care system that was never designed to replace the care and love children need from a loving parent. A crisis four years in the making is starting to erupt, but there is still time to save thousands of children and give all of them a forever family.

Chapter One

Who is Richard Villasana?

L aura Acevedo, KGTV ABC San Diego reporter:

> *"So, Mr. Villasana, you say this is going to be a daunting task for this administration to take the thousands of children who have been separated from their families at the border and to reunite them with relatives."*
>
> Laura continued, *"Would there be some children who would not be reunited with their parents?"*
>
> Richard Villasana: *"Absolutely."*

Who is Richard Villasana to be interviewed by the news about this issue of national importance?

It's June 20, 2018. I had just arrived about 12:30 p.m. at the Westin LAX Airport hotel in Los Angeles for a business function. As soon as I walked into the event, I was given the message to call ABC as soon as possible. Laura Acevedo, a San Diego ABC reporter, had been in contact with my publicity mentor, Jill Lublin.

Of course, this would be the first trip that I had ever taken in years where I was not wearing a tie. I had also been traveling for three hours. I immediately called Laura, who explained that President Trump had just signed an executive order to reunite the thousands of children who had been separated from their parents at the Mexico-United States border. ABC wanted an expert to comment on the executive order and its chances of success.

The next thing I knew I was talking to Laura about the separation of children from their families and the prospect of reuniting these children quickly. There was nothing fun about this interview. The news I needed to deliver was sobering and serious. I said:

> *"The government has a huge challenge that could take years for these children to come out of the system. This is not a quick fix. This won't happen in the next month. People need to understand that it will take a great amount of time and effort and, in most cases, years to track down relatives."*

As certain as I was of the accuracy of my responses, during the next few years this crisis would bring about surprising outcomes that I would not have imagined. As of the writing of this book, hundreds of parents have yet to be located.

Later that same day I arrived home and found an email from Jesse J. Holland with Associated Press. Mr. Holland had read several of my articles published in Foster Focus Magazine about how the foster system isn't working for Latino children. He wanted to do an article about the family separations and what might happen with those children who might not be reunited with parents and/or relatives and instead would be placed in the U.S. foster care system.

In his article, "Migrant Kids Could End Up in Already Strained Foster System," Mr. Holland highlighted two critical deficiencies with the idea of placing immigrant children in the U.S. foster care system.

> In the article I said, *"With few Spanish-speaking caseworkers, it's a challenge tracking down family members of the children who live south of the Mexico-U.S. border. Other relatives living in the States might be afraid to step forward to claim them because of fears of being detained or deported themselves."*

> I added, *"These migrant kids are going to be put into the same discriminatory system that discriminates against a Latino child because their relatives happen to be located south of the border. You've got individuals who will not pay to bring in someone who speaks Spanish, understands Spanish, can read Spanish, and knows the country and knows how to proceed in this matter, and will pick up the phone and go do this work."*

So, who is Richard Villasana and why should he be asked for his expert opinion?

The oldest of nine children, I grew up in Houston, Texas, and in my teens moved to Sugarland, Texas. The path to becoming an international authority on immigration issues and foster families began the summer after I graduated from high school.

During that summer, I took a trip through Gannon College to El Escorial, near Madrid, Spain, where I got a taste of traveling, learning about different cultures and new languages. A year later, I traveled to France and studied French at the

Sorbonne. Things accelerated for me when I moved from the Navy Reserves to active duty during Desert Storm in 1989.

I was stationed in Sardinia where I learned Italian. I received an honorable medical discharge and found myself in San Diego looking for a new career. I returned to college to complete my degree in French. It was during this time that my life's path would lead me to the career and expertise that I have now.

I'm often asked why I am so passionate about helping foster children. After all, there is not much in my teenage or early adult life where I interacted with anyone who was in foster care. On the other hand, my mom became more or less a foster mom to a couple of my friends who could have ended up being foster kids.

In high school, there may be a person's house where everyone goes and hangs out. This person was my friend Laurie Watson's home. We would all go to her house and spend time there. Her mother, Mrs. Joan Watson, was the grandmother that everyone loves. She was the sweetest person in the world. She could be stern at times but always in the nicest way possible.

When we weren't at her house, my house, specifically my bedroom, ended up being kind of a dormitory room for my friends and sometimes their friends. I had two friends in particular who stayed with me, so at times there were three guys in one room. One of my friends was going through a rough relationship with his father. At one point my friend found himself thrown out of his house at 15 years of age. After hearing this, I offered to let him stay at my house although after saying this part of me was thinking, *"What the hell are you doing?!!"* I remember calling up my mom and asking her if it was OK if he moved in.

I didn't ask my dad because, honestly, he was rarely at home, so it really depended on my mom. My dad was not around very much when I was a teenager. I remember that he would show up at home each month for a day or two throughout my years in high school. He helmed the El Patio Restaurants in Houston, Texas. At one point with 14 locations, our family had the largest family-owned restaurant chain in Houston. Even so, I really resented that he was not at home during that period.

However, looking back at that time of my life through the eyes of an adult who's married and works, I realize that he must have worked so much to provide for nine kids, keeping us in private school, having enough food in the fridge for everyone including my friends and a safe place to live. I wish I would have understood more about life and had given him a hug and told him that while I missed having him in my life, he was doing a great job.

My mom said as long as I was willing to put up with sharing my room with my friend, it was OK with her, so I got a roommate. This lasted off and on for about a year and a half. During the same time, the parents of my other best friend decided to move from Texas to the state of Georgia. Being that it was going to be my friend's senior year, I offered, and his parents accepted his living with me and my family while he completed high school. I had one other friend, and between the three of them I had at least two roommates for nearly two years.

Someone asked me one time if my friends felt like boarders, and the answer is not really. My bedroom was considered very much theirs. They lived there. They ate with my family as often as teenagers eat at home. We all worked at the local Pizza Hut together. We would get ready for Saturday night together. We partied together. Everyone was so comfortable with my house being their home that late one evening with five or six of us moving between rooms in the upstairs, we ended up having a water fight that was so bad. It was bad enough that the next afternoon when I arrived from work, I found all of our furniture stacked in the middle of the room. My friends had gone out and gotten some paint so they could repaint the walls to cover up the watermarks. My mom was so cool. She popped her head inside at one point during the repainting, looked at the walls and just said, *"Painting is a good idea."*

At age 17, I came the closest to being around people who were homeless and almost being homeless myself. I was quite rebellious, and at one point I left home mostly because I wanted to see what it was like to be on my own. All the adults, mostly teachers, kept telling me that it was hard and rough, and we students weren't going to make it unless we went to college. I wasn't really buying that. I had a full-time job. At the time I was making roughly $17,000 a year. Some of the teachers were making about that much so I quit high school and tried living on my own. It didn't work out very well for a few reasons.

If you've ever been on a budget, you know it's amazing how quickly you start to look at how much things cost, just simple things like shampoo. Have you ever run out of shampoo and had to wash your hair with soap? I had to do that one time. It's not a good look. As for rent, my manager was living in an apartment with his wife and baby son. They let me move into an extra bedroom that they had. I paid him a token amount for that room but not nearly as much as if I had gotten an apartment on my own. Things changed for the worse when Tom, a buddy of my manager, came to work at the same place. He also needed a place to stay so I lost the room since my manager and Tom had been buddies for a few years. I still had a couch to sleep on, but none of my stuff was safe from Tom grabbing and using whatever he wanted. That resulted in my waking up one afternoon, having to wash my hair before work and finding out that Tom had used all my shampoo. There simply wasn't time for me to run over to the CVS Pharmacy and buy more even if I had had the money, which I didn't have.

Ultimately, I ended up coming back home to complete my high school education. At one point I accepted that I had a choice: getting a new place to live which wasn't financially feasible or sleeping on the floor behind one of the doors at a friend's house. They did not have a lot of money and definitely didn't have an extra bed or couch. The floor was my option if I wanted a safe place to sleep. I decided at that point that it was time for Choice #3. It was time to come back home. I had had a taste of what it was like not to have a room at home and family support, working 60-80 hours a week, having to budget for transportation, food and lodging with the money that I was making. I know that thousands of foster teens who become homeless often do not have a Choice #3.

Having stopped high school and then coming back to it did confirm one thing – leaving high school didn't end my life and didn't turn into a total disaster. I believe everyone should complete high school, but I learned something very important. Adults don't have all the answers. Many teachers didn't listen to me. They just kept to the script of, *"Stay in school, go to college or else (your life is really going to suck)."* Nobody likes being talked at. We respect people who talk with us, and I respected the teachers who talked with me. We didn't necessarily agree on everything, but I appreciated that they didn't talk down to me. I realized that the "doom and gloom" that most of my teachers were pushing out was in some ways detrimental to my life education. Maybe it was their way of trying to protect me or keep me in school. Maybe they felt that if I left, I would never come back.

It would be some time before I would really start moving toward my new life in which I would locate people and ultimately specialize in becoming an international authority finding relatives of U.S. foster and immigrant children for U.S, government agencies.

This started when I entered college in San Diego. I had just left the U.S. Navy in Spring of 1993 with an honorable medical discharge and was looking to find my next career. The right thing for me to do was going back to college. Spending time in the Navy rekindled the passion I had for traveling, especially to Europe. By this time, I was fluent in French and Italian, and so I started my degree at San Diego State University. Because my degree was a language degree, nearly half of the students in my language classes were there as part of their international business degree.

I started talking to the students and finding out more about the degree. At one point I even thought about changing my degree, which was French with a minor in Spanish. I attended a lecture about international business, and that was my A-Ha experience. That was when I knew exactly what I wanted to do for the rest of my life.

The speaker was an accomplished entrepreneur who had done a lot of business in Asia. I was hearing about a career that I had dreamed existed but had never been able to find people who worked in that field. The speaker talked about traveling and meeting people from several countries and learning about different cultures. As soon as the talk was over, I ran up and started asking the speaker so many questions. He let me know that he didn't specialize in Europe, which was my goal at that particular time, and he recommended that I talk to a gentleman named Antoine Morrison. Little did I know that my meeting with him would put me on a path that I've been on ever since.

Antoine was, and still is, an amazing person. He had spent years selling wine across Western Europe as he developed an expertise in international marketing and sales. His bio said that he was a foreign market development specialist and consultant who had lived in Latin America and Western Europe for 15 years. Antoine was being modest because he is one of world's leading experts on Latin America. At the height of his career, he was negotiating multimillion dollar deals for Fortune 500 companies, the Department of Defense and other countries that wanted to do business in Latin America.

I met with Antoine, and he asked me where I wanted to do international business. I told him that I wanted to do business in Europe, but at that point I really didn't have any money. He explained that I had two choices: I could try to do business in Europe, which would be extremely difficult seeing as I had little to no money, or since I was in San Diego, California, I could do business in Mexico, which was only about twenty minutes from where I lived.

It took a couple of days for me to reluctantly accept that Mexico was much closer and would allow me to stretch out the little money that I had plus Antoine was living in Tijuana, Mexico at the time. This is where his base of operations was, and I could learn from him about doing international business. And so, I did.

At the same time, I found that I had a very unique skill in which I was able to look at documents and reports and pull out identifying information about a person on where they were living and working. Most people tend to be very rigid when they're looking at information about a person. One client wanted me to find a girl in Mexico that he had dated. Mark always regretted that they had grown apart during college and that he had not put more effort into getting back with her. Mark was very positive that his girlfriend's name had been Ania. He gave me two possible cities where she could be living in Mexico.

Mark wasn't very happy when I gave him the results of my research. The name of the person I had found was Ania Constanza. Mark kept saying that I had not found the right person, but I "knew" that I had found the right person. I had used the information that Mark gave me, but I also had followed my intuition. It told me that Ania Constanza was the right person. I told Mark to give her a call. Three days later I got a message from Mark saying that I had been right. Ania Constanza was his former girlfriend. Last I heard from Mark, he was planning to fly down to Mexico to visit her.

To me, the information I receive and the way that I process it seems very obvious, but it isn't for most people. Locating people using scraps of information and even completely wrong information is something I regarded as being very easy to do, but apparently doing the same is extremely challenging for most people. I did not realize this until later when Antoine pointed it out.

This all really started to come home for me during a trip to Mexico City with Antoine. Our goal was to find and interview distributors as we wanted to set up a network of distributors in Mexico to handle the sales of radiology equipment and products from several U.S. manufacturers.

Antoine is a very detailed individual. He had mapped out where we were going to stay and how many people we were going to interview each day. The whole trip was planned out. In addition to his list, I wanted to arrange a meeting with Jessica Jimenez, whom I had met the year before while I was in Mexico City studying Spanish. I felt we needed to meet this woman.

Antoine asked me to explain why we should go see this Jessica Jimenez, and I didn't have a good answer for him. I just knew that we needed to go see her. She was not part of our plans as we flew to Mexico City on Sunday. We stuck to the plan, visiting manufacturing sites and interviewing potential distributors. By Wednesday night, we had accomplished 90 percent of the work we had planned to do in Mexico City.

On Thursday morning, we were having breakfast inside the hotel, and I was still talking about visiting Jessica Jimenez. Antoine had previously shown me on a map that our base of operation for this trip was in the northern part of Mexico City. We would have to spend half the day traveling to the southern part of Mexico City near UNAM, Universidad Nacional Autónoma de México, the oldest university in Latin America, where this woman had her office. Antoine finally gave in and said that if we went to see this woman, he expected me to never mention her again during the trip. I agreed and off we went. We arrived at the offices for the Secretaría de Salud (Secretary of Health – SSA).

A quick primer: Mexico has three large medical institutions the handle health care for everyone in the country. At that time, Instituto Mexicano del Seguro Social, IMSS (Mexican Institute of Social Security) handled the health care for citizens who were employed. Instituto de Seguridad y Servicios Sociales de los Trabajadores (Mexican Civil Service Social Security and Services Institute - ISSSTE) also handled health care for citizens who were employed but catered to professionals such as teachers. Secretaría de Salud (SSA) was the third institution that handled health care for the poor, the elderly and anyone else who did not qualify for health care services with either IMSS or ISSSTE.

Separately these three institutions buy tens of billions of dollars of medical equipment and products every year. Any company or manufacturer looking to sell medical equipment or products in bulk to the Mexican government wants to have excellent relationships with at least one of these three institutions.

We were headed for the offices for SSA. Upon entering the building, we found ourselves looking at the board listing all of the offices and departments. Antoine started to explain how to tell who was who by looking at the directory, the board of directors, managers and VPs. Then one name caught his attention.

Pointing, he asked if this was the person, Jessica Jimenez, that we were going to see, and I said yes.

And he said, *"We're here to see this person?"*

I said, *"Yes."*

And then he asked, *"Do you know who this person is?"* and I said, *"Yes."* Antoine then gave me a look that said, *"Are you sure?"* I said, *"Maybe. Who is she?"*

It is important to remember that we were in Mexico to find distributors who would then turn around and sell U.S.-manufactured medical products to hospitals and clinics throughout Mexico.

Antoine went on to explain that if we were to sell to the government instead of through a distributor, once all the documentation had been completed, there was one person who would have to sign off on the purchase of new equipment at an institution such as SSA. And it just so happened that the one person who was signing off on billions of dollars of brand-new purchases for SSA at that time was Jessica Jimenez.

> *"Let me get this straight,"* Antoine said to me. *"This is the woman you have been talking to?"*
>
> *"Yes."*
>
> *"This is the woman that you've had cookies and coffee with, and you borrowed her books when you were here studying at UNAM?"*
>
> *"Yes."*
>
> *"Essentially this woman has been treating you like her grandson this whole time, and this is the person we are going to have our appointment with?"*
>
> *"Yes."*

Antoine was blown away because we were in Mexico City with a population of more than 21 million people, and yet I had found the one person, a very important person, at

SSA who we needed to talk to who could tell us what was going on and how to work and do business with this medical institution, which was one of the largest in Mexico, where they buy billions of dollars of new medical equipment every year.

I had not only found this woman, but I had befriended her and earned her trust so that she was loaning me her books out of her own collection, explaining to me how things worked and how to do business with the Mexican government. At this point, I knew that I could find important officials in a country, but I still didn't understand that I had a gift.

Months later, I was working with Antoine in the same office. He came by my desk and gave me a piece of paper with the name Bryan Matthews. He told me that Matthews worked for the Commerce Department in Washington, D.C., and he wanted me to find a phone number for Bryan. This was all the information that Antoine could give me. He wanted me to spend some time trying to find Matthews even though he didn't think I was going to have any success.

Later that day I walked up to Antoine's desk, and I dropped a piece of paper with a phone number on it. Antoine looked at it and asked, *"What's this?"* I explained that it was the phone number for Bryan Matthews. Antoine looked at his watch and said, *"I asked for this information five minutes ago."* I thought he was upset because I took so long. Instead, he was shocked because I had found this information in five minutes. This was before Google and before the existence of any online databases. We were still getting used to seeing WORLD WIDE WEB on Mosaic or whatever passed for a browser at that time.

Antoine told me that I could not leave his desk until I explained how I found the phone number. I explained that I called one person at the Economic Development Center. They had passed me to someone in Washington. I had talked to them for a minute. They passed me to another agency in Washington, and the woman who answered gave me the number for Bryan Matthews. I was thinking "Job done," and started heading back to my desk.

Antoine said, *"Nobody does this,"* and I stopped and said, *"Well, I do."*

And again, I was thinking "Job done," and continued walking back to my desk. Then Antoine said, *"You're not listening to me."* I had been with him for a couple of years at this point, and I knew that when he said that it meant I was missing a life lesson.

I went back to his desk and gave him my full attention. Antoine reminded me of his background, having worked for major corporations and international governments. He then said something so profound.

> He said, *"With all of this background that I have and having met people in countries around the world, when I say that nobody does this, what I'm telling you is that I have not met someone who has this ability to find someone like this."*
>
> And I said, *"I do this all the time."*
>
> And he said, *"Yes, but just because you can do it, and it's easy for you, doesn't mean it's not a valuable skill."*

This comment was so important because Antoine was the one person I trusted implicitly and when he told me this and pointed out that I had this skill, I was listening. I was ready to respond. Many times, people go through life and have a particular skill. They may think that it's a good skill or it's got some value to it, but they're not around anyone who points it out to them. Sometimes that's exactly what's needed.

We need someone to point out that one skill that we have that is so good, so specialized, so exceptional. This could be baking a cake. This could be doing research. This could be doing so many different activities, but it's an activity that we do in a such way that makes it unique and makes it superior to almost anything else that anybody else is doing in the world. And we all know some people who will not share that special gift with the world because there's not someone who knows them well enough and is willing to point this out or to whom the person is willing to listen and trust and to accept the praise about how great they are and how this thing that they do so easily is actually so valuable to people.

It wasn't much later that I started working to find other people. Originally, I had spent my talent finding government officials for work and also on behalf of other people. But then people started calling me. Professional organizations would call up and say, *"We understand that you locate people in Mexico. Can you help us locate someone?"*

It was at that point that I really started to focus on using my talent and this gift to locate people. The most fun I had, of course, was locating a relative for someone. At first it might have been someone's uncle and then the next case would be looking for someone's brother whom they hadn't seen in five to ten years. But then something very special happened. Foster care agencies started contacting and asking me to help them with cases where they needed to find a foster child's father, mother or other relatives who were living somewhere in Latin America.

One of the first foster care cases that I handled involved a former foster kid. Lorna was the oldest of three kids living with her mother in the U.S. When she was 15 years old, something happened to her mother who decided to take the two youngest children and return to her family in Guatemala. For whatever reason, Lorna was left behind. She was placed into foster care where she spent the next three years. No one in foster care had been successful in locating her mother or family in Guatemala so Lorna aged out with no family at age eighteen.

Fast forward to seven years later when her husband, Steve, contacted me about Lorna. Now in her early twenties, Lorna had started looking for her mother and wasn't having any success. Steve was a U.S. marine deployed to Afghanistan, but he cared so much about his wife that he emailed asking me to help him to find Lorna's mother and siblings.

Within about three weeks, I had located her mother, grandmother, and a couple of aunts, all living in Guatemala. Steve wrote, *"You have reunited the family. God bless you."* Doing this kind of work and reuniting families is one of most incredible feelings I have ever had.

After that time, I and a couple of volunteers started to do work for foster care agencies.

One of the first was Casey Family Programs in San Antonio, Texas. They wanted us to find a foster child's relatives. This case was extremely challenging because the only information that the agency could provide was the name of the state in Mexico and the name of the child's grandmother. To put this in perspective, this would be like someone asking you to find Mrs. Michele Johnson who lives in Texas. That was all the information that they could provide me. Even though it took a bit of effort and time, we found the grandmother in Mexico who told the caseworker about a relative who was also living in Texas about two hours away. The outcome was that the little girl was able to go live with this distant relative and get out of foster care.

One of the reasons that Forever Homes for Foster Kids is so successful is that we take each and every case and pull from them every possible detail to add to our historical database so that we can do the next case better and faster. Relationships are deepened with agencies and officials in countries throughout Latin America so that the next case that comes up can be completed more quickly, increasing the probability that the child will be reunited with relatives, or the very least, have contact with their family.

What has been the driving force that gets me out of bed every day and into my office before I had my first glass of Dr. Pepper? It's knowing that there are tens of thousands of Latino foster children in the United States and that many foster care agencies are poorly equipped to find a child's relatives so that the child can be reunited with their family. If a child is not reunited with relatives or adopted, depending upon the state, that child then "ages out" at either age 18 or 21. Instead of a birthday cake, these kids have to leave their foster home.

The future for most of these kids is becoming homeless, turning to crime so they have enough money for food and shelter, becoming a sex trafficking victim – sometimes in as little as six hours – or ending up in prison or dead often within a year of aging out. If my nonprofit and I can make a difference for just one child, that's all the motivation I need to focus my time and energies.

Chapter Two

Family Separations
at the Mexico-U.S. Border

In early spring of 2017, a massive tide of Central American immigrants was arriving at the Mexico-U.S. border on a weekly basis with the hope of seeking and gaining asylum in the United States. Many of the arrivals were children accompanied by a parent.

On April 11, 2017, Jeff Sessions, Attorney General of the United States, issued a memorandum to all federal prosecutors. It stated in part:

> *"While dramatic progress has been made at the border in recent months, much remains to be done. It is critical that our work focus on criminal cases that will further reduce illegality. Consistent and vigorous enforcement of key laws will disrupt organizations and deter unlawful conduct. I ask that you increase your efforts in this area making the following immigration offenses higher priorities. Further guidance and support of executing this priority... will be forthcoming."*

This memorandum laid the groundwork for a change in immigration policy that had never been acted upon by any U.S. administration. In the summer of 2017, this policy change would be enacted.

Throughout the following months, enormous groups of Central American immigrants continued to arrive weekly at the Mexico-U.S. border. Finally, during the summer of 2017, the Trump administration acted on its plan to discourage the increasing number of families that were coming from Central America and looking for asylum in the United States. To accomplish this, the Executive Branch took the unprecedented action of unofficially imposing a "zero tolerance" policy to Customs and Border Patrol officials along the Mexico-U.S. border. The policy was straightforward. The government would prosecute: *"100% of all parents caught crossing the border with children, whether they are crossing at a port of entry or not."*

Never before had there ever been a national effort with the quiet blessings of the presidency to treat immigrant families arriving to the U.S. through a port of entry as criminals.

Once news of these family separations reached the Central American countries, the hope was that many adults would simply feel that the cost of coming to the United States and losing their children would be too much. While the crowds did get smaller during the next several months, thousands and thousands of desperate parents still continued to travel from their country to the Mexico-United States border with their children.

During past administrations, illegal entrants would be criminally prosecuted in an attempt to reduce illegal migration, but exceptions were generally made for families and asylum seekers. Families were previously kept together. This unity was severed under "zero tolerance."

Once adults and their children were in the custody of Immigration and Customs Enforcement (ICE), the parent and child were to be separated immediately. Mothers had babies taken out of their arms. Children as young as two years old were taken from their fathers. This action was exemplified in a photo by Getty photographer and Pulitzer Prize-winner John Moore of a little two-year-old girl crying as she stood in a dusty road separated from her mother.

Thousands of other children would be taken, many kicking and screaming, from their parents along the Mexico-U.S. border. Even if a parent had told their child what was going to come next, there's truly no way for a four-year-old child to be prepared.

Imagine seeing this tableau play out for a child with a child's understanding of life. A large car or two appears suddenly in the quiet of the night in front of them and their mother. Lights are shining in the child's face, their little hands raised to block the blinding light. Then large soldiers, just like the ones that may have beaten or taken away a relative from back in their country, come out of the car. Now the child's mom is talking with these soldiers. Within several seconds, the mother is crying, maybe screaming, and a large soldier is picking the child up and stepping further away from their mother. The child is now screaming, crying.

At four years old, a child knows when something bad is happening. If their mom is struggling, now the child may believe that their mom is being attacked. The child may start to scream because to them someone is hurting and attacking their mom. Almost all children can sense when someone is upsetting or hurting their parent. A car door opens, and the child is now in the back seat of one of the large vehicles with his parent who is still upset and possibly unable to console the child.

After coming into Custom and Border Patrol custody, traumatic and forced separations happened to many of these immigrant children and their parents often within 24 hours. Other times, a parent would be taken to be interviewed only to return and find that their child was now gone. Many parents were left with no idea where their child had gone or how to contact them.

Under the "zero tolerance" policy, the Department of Justice (DOJ) was prosecuting 100 percent of adult aliens apprehended crossing the border illegally, making no exceptions for whether they were asylum seekers or accompanied by minor children. Illegal border crossing is a misdemeanor for a first-time offender and such criminal offenses can be prosecuted by DOJ in federal criminal courts.

When prosecuted by DOJ, illegal border crossers are detained in federal criminal facilities. Because children are not permitted in these facilities with adults, children under age 18 are designated as unaccompanied alien children (UAC) and treated as unaccompanied even if they were with their father or mother. The kids are then transferred to the care and custody of the Department of Health and Human Services' (HHS) Office of Refugee

Resettlement (ORR). However before "zero tolerance," these separations were rare and occurred because of circumstances such as a parent's medical emergency or a determination that a parent was a threat to the child's safety. This was a critical reason the U.S. government was spending millions of dollars contracting for new facilities to house children and parents.

Most parents were sent to a federal facility, some run by the federal government, others contracted out to third-party vendors, while children were sent to other facilities. You may have read about the terrible conditions that many adults endured once they were placed in a facility, but you may not have heard how thousands of children also suffered once they were under U.S. government care.

Asmita Deswal, the 2021 J.D. Candidate at Georgetown University Law Center, wrote this chilling summary about the Trump administration's zero tolerance policy in his paper, "Reunite Separated Families: A Call to the Biden Administration to Rectify the Impact of Trump's Zero Tolerance Immigration Policy."

> *"The policy violated international law by defying the International Covenant on Civil and Political Rights ("ICCPR"), which the United States ratified in 1992. The ICCPR mandates that the government treat persons humanely and respect the 'inherent dignity of the human person' when arresting, detaining, or imprisoning someone. It also recognizes the right to 'security of person,' 'the right to liberty,' and a right to challenge detention 'before a court ... without delay.' Forcing children to sleep on cement floors with constant light exposure, insufficient food*

and water, no bathing facilities, lack of toiletries,
portable restrooms, and freezing temperatures is
not humane. It is blatant harm to one's dignity.
The government acted with an awareness of
its culpability as Senators were denied entry into
children's shelters, and U.S Customs and Immigration
Enforcement (ICE) agents forbade reporters from
interviewing any of the detainees or taking photos."

Most Children were processed and eventually placed with a sponsor. For the most part, this word "sponsor" is just a fancy name for a relative as most of these children were placed with either the other parent who may have come up earlier and was now residing in the United States or with other adult relatives, such as an aunt and uncle. In some cases, a child was placed with a distant relative or a friend of the family. Many parents, after being processed and having spent months being in federal detention, were deported from the United States into Mexico without ever being reunited with their children. The government didn't and still doesn't seem to have a plan for reuniting all the families they tore apart.

Chapter Three

End of U.S. Government's "Zero Tolerance" Policy

The unofficial separation policy continued into 2018. On May 7, 2018, Attorney General Jeff Sessions announced that the Department of Justice had implemented a "zero tolerance" policy toward illegal border crossing, both to discourage illegal migration into the United States and to reduce the burden of processing asylum claims that administration officials contend are often fraudulent.

Nothing really changed with this announcement on May 7, 2018, with regard to the actions taken by ICE for the past year… with one very important exception. Now this policy was official. In making this policy official, after months of having to sit on the sideline, the American Civil Liberties Union (ACLU), led by Lee Gelernt, was finally able to go into federal court to file an injunction to stop the administration from separating more children from their parents at the Mexico-U.S. border.

At the same time, the family separations had garnered extensive public attention. Because of the injunction, coupled with a growing outcry from the public and politicians about the "zero tolerance" policy, the Trump administration announced on June 20, 2018, that all family separations would cease. Unfortunately, an even greater humanitarian crisis was just over the horizon.

On June 26, 2018, in a class action lawsuit brought by the ACLU, *Ms. L v. U.S. Immigration and Customs Enforcement (ICE)*, a Federal District Court ordered the federal government to identify and reunify separated families who met certain criteria. Given the potential impact of these actions on vulnerable children and ORR operations, the Office of Inspector General (OIG) conducted a review to determine the number and status of separated children (i.e., children separated from their parent or legal guardian by DHS, Department of Homeland Security) who have entered ORR care, including but not limited to the subset of separated children covered by *Ms. L v. ICE*.

The next day on June 27, 2018, I was again contacted by ABC reporter Laura Acevedo to provide expert commentary on the possibility that the Trump administration would be able to reunite the thousands of children who had been separated from their parents within 30 days.

> I said, *"The reality is that is not going to happen. That is a tall order for any administration to try to get these children who have already been shipped out to various states pulled back in and reunited with their family within 30 days."*

U.S. District Court Judge Dana Sabraw, based in San Diego, had issued an order requiring children under five to be reunited with their parents in 14 days. I explained, however, that the government could not meet this deadline.

I said, *"Not necessarily because the government isn't trying but because of the logistics, again this is just a daunting task for the government to take on."*

The June 27, 2018, Politico article focused even more on Judge Sabraw's ruling. "Blasting the Trump administration for what he called 'a chaotic circumstance of the Government's own making,' Judge Sabraw said it was a 'startling reality' that no adequate planning had been done before officials embarked on a policy to separate children from parents kept in immigration custody or referred for criminal prosecution. The practice had led to more than 2,300 children being separated from their parents or other family members."

"'The government readily keeps track of personal property of detainees in criminal and immigration proceedings,' Judge Sabraw wrote in his 24-page order. 'Money, important documents, and automobiles, to name a few, are routinely catalogued, stored, tracked and produced upon a detainee's release, at all levels — state and federal, citizen and alien. Yet, the government has no system in place to keep track of, provide effective communication with, and promptly produce alien children. The unfortunate reality is that under the present system migrant children are not accounted for with the same efficiency and accuracy as property. Certainly, that cannot satisfy the requirements of due process.'"

One of the biggest problems at the beginning with this idea of reunification was that very few people in the United States understood how the "zero tolerance" mandate had been executed. No tracking system was put into place when a parent and their child were separated. The lack of a formal tracking system created a situation where the federal government was simply not capable of meeting the ruling deadlines set by Judge Sabraw.

Jacob Soboroff in his book, "Separated: Inside an American Tragedy," expertly describes the Trump administration's lack of any cohesive plan to reunite the thousands of children who had been separated from their parents. This lack of planning would eventually lead to the humanitarian crisis that is still continuing as of July 2022.

As one of the world's leading authorities on performing family finding throughout Latin America, I can confirm that successful reunification requires skill sets and resources that the majority of agencies and their staff simply lack. Through my nonprofit Forever Homes, I've been involved in several cases with high-quality information where we were looking for a parent, and the effort took months.

For instance, we received a case where we had the parent's name, their date of birth and a street address, city and state. You're probably wondering, *"How hard could it be to find this person?"* It all depends. The first problem for this case was with the name of the parent. The caseworker only had one of their last names which was Lopez. Lopez is one of the top five most popular last names in Mexico. People in Latin American countries virtually always have at least two last names.

When an unmarried person has two last names, the first last name almost always belongs to their father with the second last name belonging to their mother. This common name structure makes doing Hispanic family research quite easy. You have a greater probability of success locating a relative who has the last two names, such as Lopez Aguilar, than searching for someone with only the last name of Lopez.

Other challenges may occur when searching for a child's female relatives such as a mother or aunt. The majority of women who marry in Latin America will take on the first last name of the husband. Let's say that an agency wants to find a mother whose name is Carmen. If she is married to Alejandro Lopez, then Carmen's last name most likely will be listed as Lopez because she is married. We could find the mother using the name Carmen Lopez, but if we knew Carmen's maiden name was Garcia Aguilar, we might be able to find other relatives. When it comes to successfully finding people in Latin America, having a person's complete name is critically important.

The second issue was with the street address. While searching for someone in the U.S. is greatly aided by having a street address, Mexico doesn't have a national database that people can access that will list street addresses. Now you're thinking, *"Just do a reverse look up."* That's a great idea for looking for someone in the U.S. Unfortunately, there is no website for Mexico where you can put in a person's address and have it give you the person's name. By now you may be getting an idea of how challenging it can be to locate someone in Latin America. There are also countries in Latin America where there are no street addresses at all.

When you're trying to find someone in Latin America, you often only know that the person lives in a particular city and state. That's all the information you usually get. That is where good family finding comes into play. Someone takes the little bit of information and is able to locate the person's contact information: street address (if one exists), city, state, zip code and especially a phone number so that organizations such as the Office of Refugee Resettlement (ORR) and foster care agencies can get in contact with this individual.

Keep in mind that the federal government had released thousands of children across the U.S. into state foster care systems. In the June 2018 Time magazine article, "'They Are Coming With Little to Nothing.' How New York City Doctors Are Treating Migrant Children," author Jamie Ducharme wrote:

> *"Indeed, roughly 700 separated children have been placed into foster care agencies in New York state… children and their government-appointed guardians have been arriving at emergency departments with 'no access to medical records' and 'no way of getting in touch with a family member to get a medical history.'"*

The LA Times was another of many news outlets across the U.S. that reported on unaccompanied children being placed in foster homes. Los Angeles received 100 such children with the majority of the children being no older than eight years old.

Multiply the above situation ten times. More than a thousand immigrant children had been spread across the country and dropped into foster care agencies under the Trump administration. Governors and state foster care agencies complained because they were receiving dozens or hundreds of immigrant children with absolutely no idea of who these children were, their medical or family history. With the passing of weeks and months, the enormous challenge to reuniting thousands of separated children with their parents would become clearer. And years later the world would see how incredibly inept the U.S. government has been in its ability to reunite those parents with their children who were separated under "zero tolerance."

Chapter Four

Challenges to U.S. Efforts to Reunite Separated Families

In the summer of 2017, prior to the formal announcement of the "zero tolerance" policy, ORR staff had observed a steep increase in the number of separated children referred to ORR care. Officials estimated that ORR had received and released thousands of separated children prior to the June 26, 2018, court order that required ORR to identify and reunify certain separated children.

HHS had identified 2,737 separated children who were in ORR's care as of June 26, 2018, and whose parents met the *Ms. L v. ICE* class definition. Additionally, from July 1 through Nov. 7, 2018, ORR received at least 118 children identified by DHS as separated.

HHS faced significant challenges in identifying separated children, including the lack of an existing, integrated data system to track separated families across HHS and DHS and the complexity of determining which children should be considered separated. Thousands of children may have been separated during an influx that began in 2017 before the accounting required by the Court, and HHS has faced challenges in identifying these separated children. Owing to these and other difficulties, additional children of *Ms. L v. ICE* class members were still being identified more than five months after the original court order to do so.

The American dream of economic opportunity and relative safety is the primary reason these parents wanted their kids to be in the United States in the first place. Mission accomplished. These parents now do not want to take any chances that could result in their children being deported.

Never seeing their child again is the price many parents are willing to pay to give their child a shot at the elusive American dream. The sad part is that the American Dream is often only an illusion for many people, both U.S. citizens and immigrants. However, just being in the U.S. is often enough for parents who come from Central America to the U.S. where there's definitely the potential for their children to have a much better lifestyle or at least a safer life away from the violence that many families suffer in their home country.

One of the primary reasons for my writing this book is that even now articles are coming out that only cover one aspect of this entire problem. One article will focus on the lack of translation services being available to Indigenous families who do not speak Spanish but instead speak a Mayan language such as Mam or Acateco. Another article may cover how one federal judge ruled that it is OK to have children as young as five years old in court defending themselves without an attorney or an interpreter. Unfortunately, it's next to impossible for a person to track and pull all these articles together to try to make some sense out of how terribly awful the situation is with how parents and children have been treated by the U.S. government for something as legally insignificant as a misdemeanor.

It is important that people have a broad understanding of what's going on and all the challenges of trying to reunite these parents who were separated from their children who are now in the United States. On Aug 12, 2021, Bill Bostock, journalist for Business Insider, wrote that the Biden officials still cannot find the parents of 337 children separated at the Mexican border by the Trump administration.

> *"Activists and US officials have helped reunited 861 children with their parents, but 337 still remain in limbo."* Bostock later references a CNN report, *"The Biden administration found that 3,913 children were separated from their parents as part of the Trump administration's "zero tolerance" policy at the US-Mexico border launched in 2018."*

One of the challenges with having a number that is so precise is that it's very likely not a real number. This is simply a number to bolster the case for the government and to pacify the public that families are being reunited and that they can show a decline in that number. In the same article, Bostock mentions that, per the ACLU, more than a thousand families were separated between 2017 and the start of "zero tolerance" in 2018. *"More than a thousand"* doesn't sound like a very solid number. The total number has shifted over the years because at times the court has decided to include families that met specific criteria while possibly removing other families. The reality is that any numbers are best guess about a mess.

Thousands of kids had gone through the federal program and been released to a sponsor, and at least their contact information had been recorded. Unfortunately, one of the biggest failings of the Trump administration was the lack of successful efforts to stay in communication with the thousands of children who were placed with sponsors from late 2017 through 2018. Some records might have had absolutely no notes meaning that nobody tried to contact the child or their sponsor in the U.S. since that time. Other records might have listed a few dates and times when a phone call was made, but the notes might also have stated that no one actually spoke to anyone. Leaving messages on voicemail does not count as making contact with a person. All voicemail tells someone is that there's a functioning phone number and not that the child or the sponsor is still living at the residence. It's also not completely unreasonable to assume that at least a few records had little or no contact information for the sponsor.

Many cases had not been worked anywhere from one to three years. Think about this. A national crisis. Thousands of families separated. And how did the U.S. government and their contractors respond to this crisis? By making a few phone calls, getting voicemail, and leaving a message? That's right. That is exactly the type of "urgent action" that some families received over a period of years going into 2020. Little to no effort had been exerted to locate some parents. More than a thousand separated Latino children will most likely remain separated because their situation isn't serious enough for the U.S. government to follow through and get the job done of reuniting as many children as possible with their families.

The sad truth is that the U.S. government with all its abilities and technology lost track of hundreds of children who were placed with sponsors as well as some of the sponsors. To counter this loss of communication, the U.S. government launched a massive effort to locate both the separated children and their parents.

There is no way to know how efficiently or correctly information was gathered from parents about their children, or from those children who were old enough to provide information themselves about who they were and where they came from. Many parents who crossed into the United States during that time had papers to prove that they were the parent of the child with them.

On the other hand, it's also true that some of those documents were completely fake. For instance, one child's father may have been living in the U.S. for a few years. The region where the family lives in Honduras may only offer a primary school education. As any loving parent, he wants his daughter to have a chance at a better future, so he asks for her to be brought to the U.S. Unfortunately, the child's mother is very ill and unable to accompany her daughter on a trip to the U.S. The child's aunt is able to make the trip, but to ensure that there will be less issues at the border, she might buy papers that identify her as the mother. It's very likely that with these documents, the aunt will not be questioned, and that entry information will be as pertaining to the mom. This deception now creates some problems when trying to find the child's mother because officials are really using the aunt's information. Of course, some adults with children arrived at the Mexico-U.S. border without any documents.

Add to this that there was no formal effort or directive to collect or copy documents that were presented to border officials or record contact information for reunification. Data gathering fell to other organizations such as ORR, which looked at reports, noticed the separations and decided to start logging and tracking this secondhand information. We do not have firsthand or good quality information from the people who were receiving the data on site at the border.

Many immigrant children are in a situation where the name of their parent is incorrect, or the information about where their parent lives is inaccurate or false. There are many reasons for these deficiencies. Even though people on the border may speak some Spanish, this does not make a border official an expert in Spanish names. Spanish names do differ from those in the United States in that people in Latin America have two last names. Some may even have more than two last names, which makes accurately listing the information challenging for someone not trained in Spanish names.

Another issue is spelling. During a November 2018 interview with CNN International, News Anchor Cyril Vanier asked me how it was possible to mess up these names. I explained that someone has to be trained in the different nuances of Spanish names. For instance, there's the last name Pina P-I-N-A, and then there is the last name Piña with a tilde ~ over the "n." This one mark makes the name completely different from the other. Names like Gonzales could end with an "S" or a "Z." There are so many different ways a last name can be misspelled, and when you have two last names, there's the potential for both last names to be spelled either incorrectly or placed in the incorrect order. If the last names are in the improper order, then the possibility of finding that person is virtually impossible without additional information. This same issue applies to first names.

There may be this belief that the people are giving this information about their names and backgrounds in a relaxed and comfortable environment. That is completely not the case, least of all for the hopeful asylum seeker. The people who arrive at the border are desperate, traumatized from their trip and during this initial interview process, an immigrant's emotional levels are probably going through the roof. They realize that their fate may rest in the hands of the individual in front of them taking their information. On top of that, the official who's taking the information is in uniform.

There are those in the United States whose defenses go up when confronted by someone in uniform such as the police. Their fear level increases significantly; their anxiety may shoot up because of past biases, prejudices, bullying and abuse that may have occurred at the hands of people in uniform. We only have to look at video footage of protests by groups such as BLM, Black Lives Matter, where police took incredibly aggressive, sometimes lethal force against U.S. citizens. Now imagine how someone who is a person of color, who has heard the stories about the U.S. police, might react having a Border Patrol agent in front of them.

Many people who come to the border are those who are fleeing violence and terrorism in their own country. Sometimes that terrorism has come at the hands of their own police, who may act with no control, and are vicious and abusive to citizens, especially women and children. These are officials who have conspired at times with drug cartels and worked for them. Therefore, people who come from Central America have no reason to have confidence in a police officer or a military official.

If anything, these people are seen as the enemy, and yet these are the people who immigrants have to interact with when they want to enter into the United States. Because of this fear, a parent may not give the proper information to a

U.S. government official. They certainly aren't in a position to feel confident about correcting an official. If that official writes down their name incorrectly, the chances are that the improper information is going to stay in place. Few asylum-seekers are going to assert themselves to explain to an official, *"Oh, you spelled my name wrong. It really should be Gonzalez with a 'z' not Gonzales with an 's.'"* It's not going to happen.

This may be a concept that's hard for the public to understand: How could officials working along the Mexico border not understand Spanish? It's not simply a matter of understanding a language. It's having a specialty in that language.

Many parents and children who came up from Central America have names that are in an Indigenous language, such as Mam. Most likely U.S. border officials lack the knowledge about these languages and names to do their jobs effectively. There are those who think of the officials at the border as heartless bastards. While that may be the case for some, the truth is that these people are at a disadvantage because they have not been trained to do this work properly.

One of the other challenges besides names not being properly recorded is that the address may also not have been recorded properly. Are the people at the U.S. border doing the intake knowledgeable about all the different structures of towns and cities in Central America? Definitely not.

There's also the assumption that all the people who are coming up to the U.S. are knowledgeable about every element of their address. Not everyone traveling up from Central America has high school degree or has studied geography enough to have a solid idea of where they're from. This is especially true if you're working with children.

If you have a child who is nine years old or younger, it's likely the child is not going to be able to offer accurate information about where they were living.

Making mistakes with information is so easy. I recently received a call from a U.S. attorney. His Latino client wanted to locate his mother who was deported from the U.S. to Mexico years ago. His client misspelled the name of the Mexican state and also gave the street address as 129 Calle Segundo. The error here is that addresses in Mexico start with the name of the street followed by the number. The correct street address is Calle Segundo 129. If you have someone entering information who does not understand the structure of street names, then you get an improper listing. Just being Latino does not guarantee that the person is providing accurate information. Misinformation gets passed to someone else who also does not understand about street names, and poor results occur. These errors continue to impact the success of locating someone in another country unless an expert in these matters is brought in who hopefully will correct the information.

It's also important to keep in mind that the names of some parents and children have been misspelled, the names provided may belong to another relative altogether (like a brother-in-law or third cousin), the names of cities and states in different countries have been misspelled and mangled or the information was completely false. This would be like someone asking you to find Mike Davis in Rio de Janeiro, California. No such city exists in the state of California.

Once you learn that a city or town does not exist in a particular state (most commonly called a departmento in Central America), the next challenge is that you now have to look at all of the possible cities, compare the names and information and see if it may still be possible to locate a parent or relative.

Just because there are nonprofits such as Forever Homes that have experience in locating relatives outside the United States, this does not guarantee success for each child. Unfortunately, we have worked some cases where even with good quality information, it still wasn't possible to locate a relative.

Even with good information, I have been involved in cases where we were looking for a parent and the effort took months. There are many reasons why a case can take this long. When you're trying to find someone internationally, you usually only know that the person lives in a particular city and state. That's all the information you have. It is very uncommon for us to get a case where someone is giving us an exact address.

Even with an exact address, the true goal is to get a phone number. Mail service in some countries is terrible and unreliable. Mail service in the U.S. can be terrible. Roughly 3.8 billion pieces of mail go and stay missing annually. Also, millions of people in Latin America have no street address.

The U.S. government has been telling the world for the last four years how critically important it is to reunite the thousands of separated children with their parents. Yet if the government failed to stay in touch with these kids and their sponsors, how serious was their effort to reunite these kids? Piss poor comes to mind.

To be fair, the Trump administration did take steps that would allow for reunification in the future. An anonymous source shared that a massive effort was launched in

2019 that targeted thousands of sponsors in the U.S. Unfortunately, this effort only resulted in locating about a third of them. Remember that if the government can't find the sponsor, then they've lost the child.

During the early months of the Biden administration, government agencies and nonprofits worked to contact parents and sponsors but again with only modest success. How bad was this situation? The title of Stef W. Kight's September 2021 Axios article says it all, "Exclusive: Government can't reach one-in-three released migrant kids." You're probably wondering, *"How is it that at that time the situation was still so terribly awful with roughly 1,500 migrant children missing?"* I'll explain.

People assume that government officials, by virtue of them being in that position, automatically know everything there is about that position, but that is not often the case. Years ago, I was working in Mexico representing dozens of U.S. manufacturers of medical products and equipment. In almost every major country, the United States has a U.S. Commercial Service office that has specialists who are assigned to a particular industry or industries. These officials are in these countries to open doors for U.S. businesses and may be in charge or oversee visits from U.S. executives who come to a country, let's say Mexico, and want to sell to the government or private businesses. These commercial officers make the introductions to influential business leaders, corporate heavy hitters. When I was doing business in Mexico in the 1990s, Antoine and I had become experts on their government bidding and purchasing process called "licitación."

During this time, Antoine and I had flown to Mexico City and met with the commercial officer in charge of the medical industry. As she was new to the position, we started asking questions and learned that she did not know how the licitación worked. We explained step-by-step how it worked. This commercial specialist was very sharp and caught on quickly once we laid out the process.

My point is that if we had not stopped in and shared our expertise with this official, there's no telling how many months would have passed before she would have been up to speed on this important process. U.S. businesses that would have spent millions of dollars to enter the Mexican medical market would have suffered by not knowing how to compete for billions of dollars in medical equipment and product sales.

Let's tie together how a commercial specialist not knowing about a country's bidding process is related to the U.S. government's inability to find roughly 1,500 immigrant children. Whatever agencies have worked on the information that was gathered together by the ORR have performed a lackluster job. You might imagine, and understandably so, that people working with immigrant children would be proficient in languages, knowledgeable about the various countries from which these children come and about their culture. You might expect these people to be able to look at spreadsheets of information and quickly pick out bad information, correct it, and then pursue all efforts to locate each child based on reviewed and accurate information. Unfortunately, that didn't happen.

It may be easy to blame the government agencies that have been involved in doing reunification. There is certainly fault with the government experts who should have done a much better job reducing inaccuracies in the information they received. But putting that aside, it is understandable that the agencies went to contractors and nonprofits to try to solve this situation. What made this crisis so much worse is that some of the people addressing this crisis were not experts in locating people in Latin America.

Many government agencies and nonprofits will simply phone in the work when it comes to handling matters internationally. These U.S. organizations usually find a company or entity in a foreign country and an all-important contact person. Then when something is needed, agencies will phone or email in their request. This probably sounds simple enough and a quick way to get things done. No one in the U.S. has to know about the nuances of each country, how the governments are structured or the correct agencies in each country that could provide an extraordinary experience or, as in the case of these separated families, collaborate to locate parents.

The downside is that these U.S. entities have little to no control over the quality of the work they receive. The contact person and foreign entity may deliver amazing outcomes, mediocre results, or an absolutely pitiful service. Since there is only one point of contact, no other options exist to get a better result.

However, it is important to acknowledge and credit at least some agencies that did look for new organizations to bring on board to assist with the reunification. At some point the involved agencies realized that they needed additional support to renew efforts or to finally launch searches to locate and contact parents in their home country. In late 2020, Forever Homes was approached to take on many cases to locate these parents.

In March 2021, we started working with the information that had been compiled over the last few years. I don't know how many government agencies had looked at the information about these children, but whichever ones they were, they did not go through the information and clean it up. I know this because when my nonprofit received several cases, we had to spend weeks of research extracting shreds of usable information from the incomplete and erroneous data we received. Because of our expertise, we were able to craft together enough reliable data to initiate a search for every parent. It's clear from the miserably poor information we received that those agencies couldn't or wouldn't put in the same effort and would continue to fail to locate parents.

The work was challenging since the recorded information was by that time two to three years old. Over the last two years, at least one organization and then our nonprofit have been successfully locating parents in their country of origin. However, inside information tells us that the primary focus has shifted back to the U.S. to find and contact the children with their sponsors. But if the goal is complete reunification for all families, this effort is going to fail. The Biden administration has been in power for more than a year and a half, so it is definitely time for it to get its political butt in gear and do everything possible to make reunification happen for these families. This happens by searching for both the parents and their children at the same time.

If U.S. officials were really informed, they would understand that finding the child does not mean you're going to find the parent. Find the parent, and you will almost always find the child. During these years of physical separation, almost all parents have been in contact with their children. Because parents are in touch with their children, it's likely that the sponsor and the child are being cautioned against providing any information to government officials that would lead them to the parent. However, find the parent in their home country, and they have the opportunity to decide if they will share their contact information and that of their child in the U.S. This two-prong approach gives the government its best chance at reuniting the largest number of families possible.

What makes locating a parent of a child who was separated at the border very challenging is that many of these parents have a great deal of fear. The fear is that if they provide their information, it will be tied to the child, and at that point the United States government will put the child on a plane and fly them to the country where their parent is living. Many parents don't want to be found. I know this because my nonprofit and I are working these cases.

Make no mistake about this – virtually no parent in Latin America wants their child to leave the U.S. and return to their country.

These parents had their son or daughter taken away, and the parent was put on a bus to a holding cell in some part of the United States. They had no idea what was happening with their children. Many parents were able to at least speak to their child, but other parents did not have the peace of mind of knowing what had happened to their child. These parents spent months in federal detention being moved from place to place. They sacrificed themselves, some enduring a lack of food and unsanitary conditions plus the anxiety of not knowing what happened with their child. These parents wanted to give their child a shot at a better life. The majority of these parents are somewhat at peace with the sacrifices they made to bring their child to the United States. And most parents live in fear that if they are found, their child will be deported from the U.S.

This is not an irrational fear. Even though the goal of the U.S. government is for these parents to be reunited in the U.S. with their child, no administration has confirmed that these children will not be susceptible to being deported. This fear is hampering most efforts to reunite these families. MSNBC reporters, Jacob Soboroff and Teaganne Finn, in their February 2, 2022, article, "White House Supports Permanent Legal Status for Families Separated at Border," wrote:

> *"The White House said this week for the first time that it backs permanent legal status for families separated at the Mexico-U.S. border during the Trump administration."*

Unfortunately, Homeland Security Secretary Alejandro Mayorkas is quoted later in this article:

> *"We are advocating to Congress that they provide these individuals with legal status — that requires a statutory change."*

Who can say with 100% certainty that before all of this is resolved, these separated children will not be deported. While I certainly applaud the above statement from Homeland Security Secretary Alejandro Mayorkas, it appears that reunification will ultimately land in the hands of a Congress that is rife with self-centered individuals and some who are openly racist and far removed from having much human compassion. However, bipartisan support is apparently what's needed to make reunification a reality. Now would definitely be a great time to offer prayers on behalf of these children and their families.

The August 2022 NBC News article, "Biden administration task force reunites 400 migrant families separated under Trump," shared a sobering statement from the ACLU. "We are thrilled for the hundreds of children who will finally be with their parents after all these years, but we are not even halfway through reuniting all the families that remain separated by the Trump administration. And indeed, we still haven't located nearly 200 families. I think the Biden administration would agree that there's a lot of work yet to be done."

Daylight is starting to peek out from this dark and dreary situation. Some of the separated parents that Forever Homes has found have now been brought back to the U.S. These families are reunited as parents bear hug their children for the first time in years.

Chapter Five

Family Finding: Foster Care's Untapped Reunification Process

Veronica is 15 years old, a typical teenager living with her father. She's thinking about her friends, maybe a crush, junior year, and homecoming. Then, boom! Her whole world changes overnight because her dad is sent to prison. Unable to be left on her own, Veronica is now in foster care, and at 15, there is almost no chance that she will be adopted. In her state, when she reaches 18, she will be put out on the street alone, with no support and no family. Veronica has a high chance of becoming homeless, turning to drugs or prostitution, or ending up in prison – all before her 20th birthday unless something happens to change her future now.

I didn't start out my professional career planning to provide a solution to the problems of children stuck in the foster care system. However, after years of working successfully in this field, nothing I have done professionally has provided more personal satisfaction as connecting these children with their families.

Most cases that foster care agencies bring to us involve U.S.-born children of at least one U.S.-born parent. However, the number of cases we handle annually involving children with family in Central and South America has been steadily increasing because hundreds of immigrant kids are coming into foster care. Our success internationally often leads caseworkers back to relatives in the United States that their agency either never knew about or was unable to locate. No matter how a child ends up in foster care, our goal, and hopefully the goal of every agency we work with, is to get these children out of the system as fast as possible.

A Dayton Daily News, Ohio May 2022 article gives a good explanation of how a child enters foster care. Craig Rickett, associate director of children services with the Montgomery County Department of Job and Family Services said:

> *"If a child or children cannot safely remain in their home, then, in order to assure that safety, we must remove them from the environment in which their safety is compromised."*

> The article explains: *"Child removal is the initial legal authorization of a public children services agency to place a child in substitute care when there are active safety threats that cannot be removed or controlled. Law enforcement can remove children from their homes and place them into the emergency custody of the local child welfare agency if officers determine that a child is at imminent risk of abuse or neglect. Kids also can be removed via a court order when the child welfare agency files a motion or complaint with the local juvenile court requesting emergency*

custody. Children are removed for abuse, neglect or dependency."

Once a child is placed in foster care, the next step always begins with family finding. The Child and Family Services Agency (CFSA) 2010 Quick Reference Guide states:

"Once the investigator or social worker has made a determination to remove the child or youth from the home, he or she shall exhaust all reasonable efforts to obtain the address and telephone numbers from the caretaker of all adult relatives and extended family members who are significant to the family and the child or youth."

The successful outcome of a family finding effort is often that a child can move out of foster care and into "relative" placement, living with family as opposed to complete strangers. "Kinship care" is the term used for this placement. Brent Chesney, a former Texas judge, said: *"Statistics show clearly that if you put someone in foster care, they stay there longer, and the case stays open longer than if you put them with a family member or a friend."*

Research by the Los Angeles-based organization Community Coalition, found that: *"children placed with relatives have better outcomes, including fewer behavioral problems, higher high school graduation rates, and less chance of unemployment and homelessness."*

Family finding is based on a simple premise: Actively identify, locate and notify as many adult relatives of the foster child as possible. Family finding is modeled after the successful process used around the world by the Red Cross. This organization goes into disaster-ridden areas where thousands of people have been separated because of natural and manmade disasters, such as floods, fires or war, and reunites family members. The concept was applied to foster care in the early 1990s.

In the identification phase of family finding, the proposed goal is to create a list of dozens of adult relatives so that at least some will have the desire and be able to take in the foster child. From this pool of family members, least one adult will step up and take in the child or, at the very least, offer to be a part of the child's life and to provide some form of family support. Many caseworkers work off a list of names provided by one or both parents. Children can also be a source of family names although they may not be able to provide specific contact information.

Once armed with a list, caseworkers then want to focus on locating these relatives. Intelius and LexisNexis® are two national databases that many agencies use to get addresses and phone numbers for relatives. Many offices have contracts with these firms so that a search of records is relatively inexpensive, in some cases less than $20 per search.

Once an agency has compiled contact information on a foster child's relatives, the next step is notification. Virtually every agency or their contracted nonprofit will mail out an official notice to each adult family member as required by law. If the agency was successful at locating dozens of relatives, then the odds are high that at least one of these relatives will respond and be willing and able to take in the child.

While it is true that not every child has relatives who will take them in, this outcome does not undermine the importance of family finding. A relative may offer to be a part of the child's life and to provide some form of family support. For those cases where relatives won't step up, the way is often cleared for that child to be adopted. At least these relatives had a chance to decide to care for this child.

Teri J. Barrett, a foster care social worker with the McDowell County Department of Social Services, probably said it best:

> *"It is painful to think that some child currently in U.S. foster care could be with blood relatives – perhaps not a perfect solution but at least one that has a chance at being humane – or, if we knew for certain that their family could not be found, we would be able to attempt a permanent placement."*

Family finding is a powerful process, and the costs are minimal compared to the phenomenal operational costs of a group home, which can reach more than $90,000 a year per child. If just twelve such foster children were reunited with a relative due to family finding, a county could save nearly $1 million a year. Those savings could then be allocated for advanced family finding training for social workers to increase the success of this process.

Other areas could also benefit from these savings as foster parent recruitment and/or retention is always a challenge for foster care agencies. If more staff were employed, then the number of caseloads per social worker could be decreased, leading to more time to visit foster children and to ensure their wellbeing.

Family finding has been part of U.S. legislation for 14 years. The Fostering Connections Act of 2008, Section 103, states:

> *"... within 30 days after the removal of a child from the custody of the parent or parents of the child, the State shall exercise due diligence to identify and provide notice to all adult grandparents and other adult relatives of the child (including any other adult relatives suggested by the parents), subject to exceptions due to family or domestic violence..."*

Many states have since passed foster care laws with similar wording – in part to qualify to receive federal funding to support family finding efforts. These states receive millions of dollars in federal aid that is then passed on to county foster care agencies and contracted nonprofits.

Based on what you just read, you're probably thinking that family finding is a well-established process in every county in the U.S., but you'd be surprised. As mentioned before, the family finding concept was developed in the early 1990s, yet nearly 30 years later no national standard exists for family finding. So, what happened?

Unfortunately, just because a law gets passed at the federal level doesn't mean that each county or even every state is adhering to the law. Let's look at some of the deficiencies.

Many county offices have some process in place for performing family finding. Some even have a well-oiled machine that does exceptional work, but other counties don't even have a formal family finding program or unit. Years ago, Forever Homes did market research and found that in California, many foster care agencies did not even recognize the term *"family finding."*

At best, it was considered some sort of activity that unknown caseworkers performed in an area hidden from the rest of foster care. Just recently a staff member in Florida shared that she had a similar experience when in 2020 she researched her state's county agencies about their family finding programs. Her own county office was just in the initial stages of setting up their program.

How do the counties obtain the needed individuals who are experienced in family finding? Not from colleges or universities. Family finding is not part of the mainstream curriculum to earn a Master of Social Work at many universities. A recent sampling of universities accredited by the Council on Social Work Education (CSWE) resulted in none of the universities offering course work on family finding.

One administration official commented that students take courses on interacting with children and families, but family finding was not directly mentioned nor was there a description mentioning this process. The prestigious Columbia University is one of many that has a well-developed master's program yet has no course work on family finding. UC Davis had a seminar years ago with a focus on family finding, but one seminar is far from providing a solid understanding of the merits of this important process. Education in family finding for staff often falls on the shoulders of each foster care office.

With no national standards of practice, many agencies have had to design their own family finding training, but an enormous problem with family finding involves the lack of training for caseworkers. Marcia Lowry, director of Children's Rights Inc., said during an interview with ABC News:

> *"Most of the caseworkers in this country are inadequately trained, do not have the educational background to do the job and have caseloads too high for any human being to handle no matter how well-trained they are."*

Many social workers handle 50 or more cases per month, an impossible task that could and often does crush the spirit. Janet Atkins, a California social worker for child-protection agencies, added, *"There's no way you can see 54 children once a month and still do the rest."*

But wait! Some caseloads are so much worse. The Feb. 2022 article headline of Tampa Bay Times reporter, Christopher O'Donnell, says it all: "154 Kids, 1 Casework Manager: Hillsborough's Foster Care Staff Crisis."

> The article continues: *"'What is happening in Hills borough is also happening across Florida as counties struggle to retain and recruit foster care case managers. Nearly 600 case manager positions statewide — around 40 percent of the budgeted workforce — are either vacant or filled by someone who hasn't completed the necessary training to manage cases,' said Kurt Kelley, president of the Florida Coalition for Children."*

Many counties across the United States have found a solution around the lack of staff by contracting their family finding services to nonprofits. The Children's Service Society of Wisconsin handles this process for their state's foster children while other nonprofits perform this work for their local or regional counties. Casey Family Programs and Seneca Center are two national organizations that also provide family finding within the U.S.

The advantage for county foster care agencies is that these nonprofits often perform with a higher level of success because family finding is a key focus of the organizations. These nonprofits have staff with years of experience as well as the budget and resources to handle the incoming case load.

Clif Veneble is an authority with 15 years of experience performing domestic family finding for the National Institute for Permanent Family Connectedness at Seneca Family of Agencies. He shared:

> *"Research over the last 20 years has proven beyond a doubt that placing foster children and youth with family members instead of in the foster care system is a better option for counties and states, and more importantly, for the child. I've found that in the vast majority of cases there are relatives out there that are ready and willing to play a part in the child's life. In the past, agencies have struggled with finding the time and resources to locate family members, but these days, even with international searches, particularly in Latin America, there are resources out there to help quickly and efficiently locate extended family members for youth in care."*

Unfortunately, hundreds, maybe thousands, of counties are keeping their family finding in-house where it either isn't embraced or executed at a high level of proficiency.

Another critical problem that negatively impacts a county's success is the moving of family finding money to other programs. Too many counties place their focus on "bright, shiny" new programs, such as transitional housing and mentoring, and investing the major portion of funds in foster and adoption programs. These are certainly important programs because not every child has a relative or gets adopted before they age out. However, foster care agencies will continue to fail tens of thousands of children who enter the system who could be placed with their families rather than spending most of their childhood in a government system.

A result of the diversion of these funds is that some agencies don't notify every relative they locate. An anonymous source shared that she was in a meeting with a foster care director. A caseworker came in to review the list of relatives they were going to notify. The director told the caseworker to send out one notice to only one family member because it would take too much time and cost to send out the notifications to all the relatives. I only know this because someone was willing to share this personal experience with me. Unless there is a whistleblower in each office, it's extremely difficult to know how often counties cut corners and cost by reducing a foster child's chances of being placed with a relative. I'd lay odds that thousands of relatives are never contacted who would gladly take in a child if they were only notified.

Given the situation where experienced staff is performing the work properly, family finding for a foster child's relatives who are living in the U.S. is quite successful. Some counties and agencies boast a success rate of up to 85 percent. Unfortunately, these numbers drop dramatically when it comes to Latino foster children.

The Pew Hispanic Research Center reported a population of 62.1 million Latinos in the United States in 2020, with nearly 59 percent being of Mexican origin. According to Child Welfare Information Gateway, 91,146 Latino children made up one-fifth of all foster kids in 2019. More than 56,000 Latino foster kids probably have an absent birth parent, a grandparent or other adult relatives in Mexico who are far beyond the reach of U.S. search engines.

Conducting international family finding results in similar benefits as performing family finding domestically. However, anything done internationally comes with additional challenges to achieving success when a service is performed in another country. Additional training, expertise and resources are critically important to performing family finding throughout Latin America to ensure the best chance at success.

I founded **Forever Homes for Foster Kids** precisely because so many foster care agencies lacked the resources or trained staff to perform international family finding. My charity is veteran and Latino-owned and specializes in family finding throughout Latin America including Argentina, Brazil, Honduras, Mexico and the Dominican Republic. For nearly 30 years, Forever Homes has taken on cases from government agencies, nonprofits and law firms working on behalf of foster care agencies or a foster child.

I've helped more than 11,000 children, adults and families reunite with their relatives in Latin America. We've worked for the U.S. Department of Defense to locate relatives of a service member and have also reunited U.S. service members with their relatives in Latin America. We have performed family finding for nonprofits such as the YMCA and Casey Family Programs as well as for various offices of CASA.

CASA of Travis County, Texas, brought a case to Forever Homes involving two siblings in foster care. By the time we got this case, the older sister had already aged out of foster care and was on her own. Child Protective Services (CPS) had not been successful at finding relatives of these children. The fear was that in several years the brother would also be forced out of foster care, and both would spend the rest of their lives with no family other than each other to help them. CASA had some information on relatives possibly living in Mexico and hoped that our nonprofit could find them.

A CASA family finding specialist wrote, *"The child has had no contact with family members for a number of years and has suffered greatly because of it. Unfortunately, we occasionally have a case that gets 'stuck,' for lack of a better word. This happens when we use all of the resources that we have but are still unable to locate positive supports for a youth. With this particular case that Forever Homes for Foster Kids was handling, the youth knew she had family in Honduras but had lost all contact with that family."*

We knew that if we found at least one adult family member, it would change the lives of these two siblings forever. Within a few weeks, we were able to provide the CASA with contact information. She was then able to call and talk with the children's birth father as well as with several other adult relatives, all living outside of the United States.

The family finding specialist also learned that these foster children had an aunt living in North Carolina and passed that information to CPS. About our success in finding these family members, the specialist wrote, *"We feel confident that we will be able to reconnect these siblings with their relatives and instill hope in a hopeless situation."*

You may be thinking, *"But it's going to cost so much money to find those relatives internationally."* The argument that it's too costly to locate relatives of a Latino foster child is groundless. Family finding is one of the most economic activities that exists in foster care. Kern County's California Permanency for Youth Project stated in a 2008 report:

> *"Over $200,000 a month could be saved if only 37 youth were placed [with relatives], resulting in millions in annual savings. The calculations provide solid cost justification for permanency programs, aside from the immeasurable benefits that come from providing youth with homes."*

Each year a child spends in a group home can cost $84,000 or more. These numbers are supported in the decisive report, "Institutions vs. Foster Homes: The Empirical Base for a Century of Action," by Richard P. Barth at the Jordan Institute for Families, School of Social Work, which states:

> *"The costs of institutional care far exceed those for foster care or treatment foster care. The difference in monthly cost can be six to 10 times as high as foster care."*

So, let's say it costs $2,000 to find a child's relatives in Latin America. For the $84,000 that would be spent on a single year of foster care for one child, the relatives of 42 children could be found, saving the state a little more than $3.4 million per year.

Maybe you're still wondering, *"Why should U.S. tax dollars go to pay for family finding when a parent is living outside the United States?"* Another excellent reason is that an appeals court could overturn a TPR (a ruling for Termination of Parental Rights) or a subsequent adoption of this child. Judges generally adhere to the legal requirements of notification in the FCA. This is exactly what happened in a case in which a Texas Appellate Court reversed a TPR on the grounds that the father, who lived in Mexico, had not been properly served notice of the state's intent to terminate his parental rights. Imagine the thousands of dollars wasted by both CPS and the court in conducting a TPR that now has to be retried at additional expense to CPS and the court. The difference in cost between conducting the mandated family finding and the court costs incurred are significant.

Some adoptions can get held up for many months or more than a year because the court wants to ensure that a thorough family finding is performed to locate a child's parent. A TPR is often needed so that the way is clear for a foster child to be adopted. Detailed family finding will either locate the parent, who can then decide to be a part of the child's life or give up their rights, or not find the person. In those cases where the person cannot be found and based on a sound report, most judges will rule for the agency to begin the TPR process. The most likely outcome is that the foster child will now have a forever home.

Family finding most often produces positive life-changing results for foster children whether done domestically or internationally and economic savings for agencies so that budget dollars can be applied to other areas.

So why is it so challenging for foster care agencies to do family finding for Latino foster kids? Four critical problems cause thousands of Latino foster kids to never be reunited with their families. These problems are the lack of: Spanish speaking staff, training and resources, belief, and most importantly, accountability.

Lack of Spanish speaking staff is a huge issue for many foster care agencies. Without someone who understands, reads and speaks Spanish, agencies are at the mercy of organizations that provide translation services. These services can be very costly and may take days to put in place before a caseworker can talk to a parent or child. Agencies also have to contend with other issues when a case involves a Latino child. Legal documents are often in Spanish. The names of family members will probably be in Spanish, and they will have two last names.

Few caseworkers read or understand Spanish. To give you an idea of how critical the situation can be, a grand jury in 2011 delivered a scathing report about the Napa County, California child welfare services. In a county where one-third of the residents are Latino, the agency only had two employees who were bilingually certified. Eleven years later, many counties across the country are struggling to have even one Spanish-speaking caseworker. We recently received a call from an agency where their one and only Spanish-speaking caseworker had left, and the new caseworker doesn't speak Spanish.

Now let's add the international component and the lack of training and resources. Most states have woefully inadequate procedures in place to locate relatives of Latino foster children internationally. During interviews, several U.S. family finding specialists and supervisors have commented about struggling and "hitting a wall" when it comes to locating relatives in Latin America. Some officials have been more candid in saying they have "no idea" how to find these family members. Dedicated social workers often experience frustration when they attempt family finding in Latin America because they lack the training and/or resources to succeed.

Here's a sample of an inquiry Forever Homes might receive from a county foster care agency.

> *"I have a referral for a child whose grandfather may be in El Salvador although no one knows for sure. It was a short-term relationship with the grandmother who is now dead. The grandfather's name is common and may have one of two different spellings, Alfonso Mendeola or Mendiola. I do not know what area of El Salvador he is from or how old he is. I am wondering what kind of help your organization could provide. The child is about to go up for adoption in a non-Hispanic home, and I am concerned that Child Welfare has not found any Hispanic relatives for this child. Thank you."*

It would be perfectly understandable if this case worker was a little frustrated and discouraged. One of the challenges with doing international family finding is that caseworkers and management need to believe that there's be a chance of success. I often use the example of a case where a foster child's relatives are living in Tanzania in Africa. A foster child's U.S. caseworker might not pursue the matter because to them this country seems so distant and inaccessible that the caseworker couldn't imagine successfully locating any relatives.

Commentary from the U.S. federal government does not help the belief level of caseworkers and management. The government has often taken an insulting attitude toward its Latin American neighbors. Its dehumanizing rhetoric about the people in Latin American countries and their "corrupt" governments makes it understandable that some, if not many, in social services view performing family finding in Latin American countries to be futile – a waste of precious money and time.

Yes, there are some challenges for foster care agencies, but now let's get real. State and federal laws require each foster care agency and their contracted nonprofits to perform family finding for each foster child. That's it. Solutions exist to help foster care agencies with international family finding at least in Latin America. Foster care agencies don't have to spend thousands of dollars ramping up efforts to do family finding abroad. Just as they do for family finding in the United States, counties can contract out the work. Cases that can appear hopeless to an untrained caseworker or manager can have very successful family finding results when done by a nonprofit with experience and resources. Other agencies could choose to bring in experts to sharpen up an existing family finding program with the proper training. Many foster care agencies don't know services are available to help them with family finding, but with the proper motivation they will search until they find the help they need. New agencies and nonprofits contact Forever Homes every week.

You may be thinking that agencies will search for an organization or nonprofit to help them with Latino foster kids because that's the law, but that's not happening because of the lack of accountability. Without family finding, thousands of Latino foster children will have no chance to connect to their families for years maybe never. Family finding is a primary function of every foster care agency.

Why then is it that these cases don't often go anywhere, and no one is likely to be reprimanded, written up or lose their job? Why do so many foster care agencies treat family finding, especially internationally, like it's optional rather than a legal requirement? To understand why no one is held accountable for not performing family finding for a child, you have to know that the federal government is to blame because it gave the Fostering Connections Act (FCA) a loophole. When a federal law is passed, it is either assigned guidelines or regulations, but a law that is assigned guidelines is a toothless law. No accountability is tied to a guideline. After years of effort to get legislation passed to improve family finding, the FCA was given guidelines.

The feeble guideline put out by the U.S. Department of Health and Human Services, Administration on Children, Youth and Families states:

> *"We encourage the agency to develop protocols for caseworkers that describe the steps that should be taken to identify and notify relatives when a child is removed from his or her home. Further, we encourage the agency to go beyond this requirement to specify ways to identify and work with relatives when the agency first becomes involved with a child at risk of removal."*

That's it. Foster care agencies are "encouraged" to do the right thing.

When there is no accountability, there is little or no motivation to perform according to procedures. To simply rely on people doing the right thing – well, have you ever seen anyone drive faster than the posted speed limit? Those signs of encouragement don't usually do much to slow down traffic. One could say that the police offer an occasional incentive to drive the speed limit because the accountability for getting caught speeding could be a costly ticket. Believe it or not, this speeding scenario has more accountability than breaking the FCA requirements of having *"to exercise due diligence to identify and notify all adult relatives of a child's removal from his parents within 30 days of that removal."*

Repercussions from one's actions exist to keep people from doing crazy, dangerous things that could harm themselves or others. While the risk of punishment does not detour everyone, having to be accountable for one's actions does work for most people. The same is true for workers in any industry. When there is no accountability, maintaining quality is very challenging, much less improving upon it.

Sad to say that in too many foster care agencies, a Latino child isn't seen as being as deserving as a non-Latino child, and it appears that many agencies have decided that Latino kids aren't worth the effort to find their families. You're probably thinking, *"Hey! What about Forever Homes or someone else?"*

Remember I mentioned that many foster care agencies allocate a significant portion of their budget to foster parent recruitment and retention? I also mentioned that many agencies move funds they receive specifically for family finding to other areas of foster care. Bottom line: agencies will say that they do not have any money to afford international family finding. Not that this is any better, but many agencies give the same excuse to nonprofits that provide family finding within the U.S.

Forever Homes offers its international services to U.S. counties and nonprofits pro bono (free). We decided to do this years ago because we got so fed up listening to foster care agencies say that they could not afford to pay a few hundred dollars for international services. To put this into perspective, I have been paid more for half an hour of my time consulting with a client on international marketing than the amount we were asking foster care agencies to pay. The truth is that's pretty sick.

Family finding is not the only solution for foster kids, but it is a powerful tool that is too often not used to its fullest potential – or worse, is treated as a suggestion rather than the obligation that each caseworker and foster care agency should be bent on fulfilling especially for Latino foster children.

You may be thinking that at least Latino foster children are being placed with appropriate foster families. That's not happening. Non-Latino foster families who speak Spanish or understand the culture are in very short supply. While counties across the country are always in need of more foster parents, virtually every county will always have a serious deficit of Latino foster parents. One of the big reasons for the deficit is the Latino culture itself.

Family is a huge part of being Latino, but what most non-Latinos don't understand is that when we say family, we're talking about "Family." Generally speaking, Latinos are dedicated to their own family first, but they are always helping other family members. This means for a couple that has a child or two, their first responsibility is to their own family, but that responsibility may also include helping a mother-in-law who is in need of time, care, or financial support. It could mean giving money to help a niece. If a family has enough funds, that money may be expanded to help grandchildren, cousins and other relatives who may still be living in Latin America.

A Pew Research Center study revealed that in 2016 *"in Latin America and the Caribbean – together making up a region where many people say economic conditions are bad – remittances rose to $74.3 billion."*

This is how family functions with Latinos. Because every Latino family has this large extended family, by the time they have spent all their resources and done everything they can to provide for their own immediate and extended family, there is little to give to someone else's family.

The idea that Latinos in large numbers will want to adopt or to become foster parents doesn't work because many only have enough time and money to cover their own family's needs. This means that many Latino children who come into the foster care system end up being placed with non-Latinos who don't understand their language or culture.

Foster care agencies are legally mandated to perform family finding. Doing anything less by a government agency can only be taken as refusing to do one of the most fundament activities for a foster child – helping that child get out of the system as fast as possible. No caseworker, director or anyone in the public should accept any excuses for this not taking place.

Happy endings require effort. Fortunately, some counties and nonprofits do put in the work to get wonderful results.

As for Veronica, the 15-year-old mentioned at the beginning of this chapter, she's no longer in foster care. We found her birth mother, grandmother, and several other relatives. Veronica's mother gave the caseworker contact information about two aunts who are living in Los Angeles. Veronica now lives with her aunts and has gone back to thinking about college and whatever else a teenager does with a future full of possibilities.

Veronica's story is foster care at its best. Yet you can't win if you don't play or even try. Incoming immigrant kids to the foster care system will only add to the number of Latino children who each year will not have a chance of having a forever home until many more agencies do family finding. Foster kids deserve a system that works diligently from the get-go to give them a loving family and to make more of these success stories possible. It's time for the U.S. foster care system to deliver.

Chapter Six

Discrimination of Latino Children in U.S. Foster Care

M ost states are simply doing a token effort to satisfy the legal requirements of family finding. While indisputable evidence that agencies are doing second-rate family finding on behalf of Latino foster children is difficult to prove, our experience, and that of other agencies, reveals that Latino foster children are being discriminated by the foster care industry. If the federal government, with all its vast resources, presents organizations such as ours with information that is so inaccurate and incomplete, how likely is it that county agencies are doing a superior job with high staff turnover rates, ongoing budget issues and caseworkers that lack training and resources?

When it comes to Latino children, some foster care agencies and nonprofits are prejudiced against doing the work that they're contracted to do. I've already covered the deficiencies at the federal, state and county level in performing a thorough family finding to locate a child's relatives in Latin America. Let's also not forget about the lack of accountability due to the FCA being assigned guidelines instead of regulations.

Besides trying to find relatives, the other part of the family finding equation is Engagement. The family members who have been notified and respond with interest to reunite with a child go through a vetting process called Engagement. Caseworkers will work with family members to receive required documents about the relatives. Staff in many foster care agencies usually perform this activity at an appropriate level when it involves a white or non-Latino child. Even for Latino children, the outlook should be fairly optimistic if the process is done correctly.

A child's family members still living in Latin America almost always know of a relative or close family friend in the U.S. who will take in the child... if they are notified. The relatives whom my nonprofit located in one case were living in Guerrero, Mexico and eagerly informed the caseworker that the foster child had an aunt living in Austin, Texas. The outcome of another case resulted in the relatives who were living in Honduras sharing contact information about a godmother living in Northern California. She not only took in the foster child but adopted him a year later.

Unfortunately, a foster care agency can still experience challenges when dealing with relatives living in Latin America. Engagement requires agencies to have staff who speak Spanish or, increasingly so, a Mayan language so they can communicate with these family members. Forms that relatives need to fill out now have to be in Spanish, and someone must have the ability to read and understand the information in Spanish received from relatives.

Just because someone speaks English well as a second language does not mean that they are able to review contracts and legal documents with a high level of proficiency. When was the last time you looked over a 30-page insurance policy and didn't have any questions or didn't find out until it was too late that you gave up the naming rights to your first born when signing documents for a new car? You or someone you know has probably been negatively impacted by some fine print in a contract that was overlooked or not understood.

While searching for a child's family members in Latin America, we have encountered some interesting situations. In one case we were working with an official to locate an uncle. Our communication was always in Spanish. Once we found the uncle, he explained in broken Spanish that he mainly spoke the Mayan language Acateco. We were able to pass along important information to the uncle because the official working with us also spoke Acateco.

In other cases, we have passed along information in Spanish to a foster child's relatives in Latin America. However, sometimes it is necessary for a caseworker to have a phone conversation with a relative to review the information in the letter. Again, just because information is in a person's first language doesn't mean that they understand everything that they're reading or all the implications.

Unfortunately, many immigrant parents did not receive information in their first language or have anyone available to help them understand the documents they were reading. In the August 2018 Associated Press article, "Complaint: US Officials Coerced Migrants to Sign Documents," reporter Astrid Galvan wrote:

"A complaint filed against the Department of Homeland Security on Thursday alleges many parents were coerced into signing paperwork they didn't understand and that they were verbally and emotionally abused while detained and away from their children."

Certainly, immigrant children received better treatment than their parents. Once again, the U.S. government disappoints. Christina Jewett and Shefali Luthra delved into the horrible actions of the U.S. government in their Texas Tribune June 2018 article, "Immigrant Toddlers Ordered to Appear in Court Alone." The reporters quoted Lindsay Toczylowski, executive director of Immigrant Defenders Law Center in Los Angeles:

"We were representing a 3-year-old in court recently who had been separated from the parents. And the child — in the middle of the hearing — started climbing up on the table. It really highlighted the absurdity of what we're doing with these kids."

The article revealed that immigrant children, most if not all who did not speak English, were having to appear before an immigration judge to explain the reason they should not be deported. The article also pointed out that this practice existed before the Trump administration.

A recently released U.S. Department of Justice (DOJ) document addresses several complaints it has received:

"alleging race, color, and national origin discrimination in the child welfare system. These complaints include allegations that such discrimination has resulted in: biological parents being denied equal access to

culturally competent reunification services; denial of relative or kinship placements; unnecessarily long stays in foster care; and family members being denied full and informed participation in family courts and social services simply because they have limited proficiency in speaking, reading, writing, or understanding the English language."

The document goes on, *"Title VI states: 'No person in the United States shall, on the ground of race, color, or national origin, be excluded from participation in, be denied the benefits of, or be subjected to discrimination under any program or activity receiving federal financial assistance.'"*

The majority of Latino foster children are U.S. citizens and not the children who are reported to have been brought across the Mexico-U.S. border. The only "crime" these foster kids have committed is being Latino. As such, these U.S.-born kids are definitely entitled to their civil rights. Title VI of the Civil Rights Act of 1964 makes it illegal to discriminate against someone on the basis of race, color, religion, national origin, or sex.

The civil rights of tens of thousands of Latino foster children are being violated specifically because of their ancestry, their national origin. An official with the U.S. Department of Justice, Civil Rights Division, admitted to me in a private conversation that the rights of Latino foster youths are likely being violated. The worst part is that as far as we know, no Latino organization or politician has stepped up to address these civil rights violations on behalf of the Latino children in foster care.

The DOJ document continues: *"Intentional discrimination occurs when the recipient acts, at least in part, because of the actual or perceived race, color, or national origin of the alleged victims of discriminatory treatment. To prove intentional discrimination, one must show that the challenged action was 'motivated by an intent to discriminate.' Evidence of discriminatory intent can be direct or circumstantial, and ill-will is not required. Such evidence can be found in, among other things: statements by decision-makers; the sequence of events leading to the decision at issue."*

The last statement is so significant. Immigrant families and their children experience varying forms of intentional discrimination as do thousands of U.S. Latino foster children. Normally the only way to detect outright discrimination and prejudice is to be in a situation where one sees it firsthand such as a caseworker hearing derogatory comments from a colleague. On the other hand, "discriminatory intent" is easier to detect in foster care agencies and nonprofits by the omission of actions that they take. Those in my organization have observed intentional discrimination while interacting with some foster care agencies. While I cannot talk about the treatment that other minorities receive in foster care, I can confirm that a simply obscene level of prejudice and ignorance exists in the foster care industry when it comes to Latino foster children.

One of the instances of Title VI civil rights discrimination that my nonprofit and I encountered started with the receipt of the following email sent in October 2017 by Alex, a foster teen under the care of a Northern California county.

"I haven't seen my father since I was three. I have little info on him. He was born in Mexico, and I have a picture of him. I know it's limited, but I am trying to find him, and I need help. So please could you help? You can contact my social worker. Thank you."

Foster care agencies have certain federal and state mandates when it comes to a foster child's parents. Knowing the whereabouts of both parents is critically important because the laws have been written to protect the rights of parents. Lack of this information deeply affects various aspects of their children's lives ranging from their daily diet, medical visits, school attended and outside activities.

For example, California Regulations under the Welfare and Institutions Code 302 (b) state:

"Unless their parental rights have been terminated, both parents shall be notified of all proceedings involving the child... The social worker shall also provide both parents, whether custodial or noncustodial, or any guardian, or the counsel for the parent or guardian a copy of the report prior to the hearing, either personally or by first-class mail."

Every state has a similar law stating that both parents have the right to be notified about the care of their child who is in foster care. To provide this notification, both parents must be located and notified when their child is placed in foster care. Nothing in the law overtly states that the requirement of notification is waived because a parent lives outside the U.S.

Unfortunately, tens of thousands of Latino foster children are not so lucky. Despite being U.S. citizens, these kids often have a parent who is now living outside the United States in Latin America. While some foster kids can provide their caseworker with names, addresses and phone numbers of relatives in the U.S., many others have little to no information about their family members living in the U.S. or abroad.

Depending on the age of the child and how much information a child can provide, agencies must often rely on getting critical information from a parent. To make matters even more challenging, a parent may, as some do, provide inaccurate information on the whereabouts of the other parent or their relatives.

Alex's email included his caseworker's phone number. We had never received an email directly from a kid still in foster care. I decided to oversee this case personally. I spoke with the caseworker, who was shocked, even embarrassed, that this foster teen had emailed us. I explained that we would take on the case pro bono. The caseworker was extremely enthusiastic. All of this happened in October 2017. We expected to receive the case information about the father so we could get started. We followed up a few times but had not received any case information. We talked with the caseworker in early November, but nothing came in. Thanksgiving passed. Christmas season came, and the caseworker seemed to be on vacation because we could not reach him. This wasn't too unusual or seen as a red flag. Staff in many U.S. agencies will take off from the third week in December and won't return to work until the first full week of January.

We had not heard back from Alex's caseworker by the second week of January. We followed up several times without any response. Sometime in February, we got a call from someone who identified themselves as the new caseworker for Alex. We gave her the same information that we had given to the first caseworker. She was equally enthusiastic about receiving our help with the case, and once again we waited to receive information about Alex's father so we could get started.

A month went by, and we still had not received any information about the father. I decided to contact the agency personally. I was passed to the supervisor. She didn't initially recall the particulars about Alex's case, which was completely understandable as caseworkers take on many cases. I explained once again about the case and our providing family finding services pro bono. I was anticipating that this supervisor would be enthusiastic about having my nonprofit search for Alex's father in Mexico free of cost.

It is important to keep in mind that the Foster Connections Act of 2008 and the family finding process almost take as a given that foster care agencies will look for both parents. Most states have laws that require foster care agencies to contact both parents unless a judgment by a court precludes notification. All Alex wanted was someone to do the minimum, find his father. The supervisor was being offered expert international family finding to be performed for free. This was a no-brainer. A slam dunk.

Yet in a matter of minutes the conversation went from the supervisor being unfamiliar with Alex's case to her telling me, *"We have decided not to pursue this matter."* Within a five-minute phone call, this supervisor committed intentional discrimination against Alex.

Let's not forget that months had gone by, and this agency had not yet found Alex's father. It was clear that this agency lacked the expertise, and most likely the will, to look for

Alex's father. This supervisor violated both state and federal laws by deciding that she would not engage in family finding for this foster teen.

That conversation still angers me today. Alex, if you hear about this and still want someone to look for your father, email or call me, and I will look for him personally. That's a promise. And to Alex's foster care supervisor, *"Rot in Hell!"* There is no way to know how many other Latino foster children were mistreated, discriminated and had their civil rights violated in the same way under her watch.

Another terribly sad part of Alex's story is that he probably has some relatives already living in the United States. He could have left foster care and been spending his teen years with loving family members. The family finding process requires that somebody at a foster care agency has the training, resources and linguistic skills to work with Latino relatives and walk them through the Engagement process so that a child can be placed with the family. More importantly, though, family finding demands that a foster care agency has staff and management who care enough to do what's best for each foster child.

Some foster care agencies across the United States are challenged to perform the Engagement process effectively in English. If these agencies lack the expertise and resources to properly do Engagement in English, then how can we expect that they're going to be able to come up with a streamlined process when it comes to Engagement with Spanish-speaking families?

At the end of the day, foster care agencies are still legally required to *"provide notice to all adult grandparents and other adult relatives of the child."* Yet thousands of Latino foster children are most likely being discriminated against because agencies are either not performing family finding or are doing sloppy work out of prejudice because of these children's national origin. In either instance, the civil rights of these foster children are being violated, and each week an unknown number of immigrant kids are passing out of federal programs and into county foster care systems across the country creating a new crisis of discrimination.

Chapter Seven

U.S. Government's Reunification Incompetence

In September 2021, the Department of Homeland Security launched two websites, together.gov and juntos.gov. These sites were directed specifically at the parents who had been separated from their children. On some level the reasoning made sense. In Sales, one of the most important mantras is, *"Make it easy for the customer to say yes."* Someone in the government probably thought, *"Let's make it easy for parents in Central America to give us their contact information by going to a website."* The government even put up a separate website with all the information in Spanish. A few parents probably did fill out the form.

However, if the goal was to draw in the still separated parents of more than 1,200 immigrant children, then this was an effort doomed to failure. Statements such as *"You may qualify to begin the reunification process and receive support services."* and *"The Family Reunification Task Force will determine whether you qualify to file an application with Task Force support."* are not very reassuring. This is nothing more than telling people that they may win the lottery but only if they pay and play.

While the creation of these two sites was well intended, it once again completely missed the mark. One overarching reason efforts to locate separated parents and confirm their contact information have failed is that few parents are going to risk their child's future of living and working in the United States because of something that sounds like a sales pitch to play Powerball™.

The other problem is with websites themselves. Government agencies throughout Central America share casual and important information through their social media accounts because the news can easily be updated to stay current. The money for the U.S. websites would likely have been better spent on efforts to locate the parents in their home country or putting out updates through a social media page to match the communication style these parents are used to.

Do these parents truly have any reason to be concerned about giving out their information? Absolutely!

Keep in mind that after four years of being in the U.S., hundreds of these children are nearing twenty-one years of age, meaning they will legally be adults. They could easily find themselves deported to Latin America. You only have to look at how the U.S. has treated DACA (Deferred Action for Childhood Arrivals) children to know that deportation to Latin America for some of those separated immigrant children is a probability unless legislation is in place to protect them.

Between 1980 and 1994, roughly 22 million immigrants entered the U.S. mostly from Mexico and Latin America. Families, including their children, who entered the U.S.

without proper documents have been at risk of deportation at any time. In June 2012, former Secretary of Homeland Security Napolitano issued the DACA memorandum halting or deferring the deportation of these children. Since that time, more than 825,000 immigrants have enrolled in DACA, but policies can change even without Congress or the White House. On July 16, 2021, the U.S. District Court for the Southern District of Texas held that the DACA policy "is illegal." However, children and adults who were in the DACA program on or before July 16, 2021, are protected for now.

DHS (Department of Homeland Security) will continue to grant or deny renewal of DACA requests, according to existing policy, but those granted exceptions have it for only two years. Even under DACA, a person is eligible to be deported if they have been convicted of a significant misdemeanor, or three or more other misdemeanors, and do not otherwise pose a threat to national security or "public safety." Of course, what constitutes a threat to public safety is completely arbitrary. A 21-year-old who has spent almost all their life in the U.S. could be deported for as little as having crossed a solid white line on the freeway, having a broken head light and an expired license. While government documents say that a driving misdemeanor doesn't count, it also states that a person's *"entire offense history can be considered along with other facts to determine whether, under the totality of the circumstances, you warrant an exercise of prosecutorial discretion."* Finally, DACA does not confer lawful permanent resident status or a path to citizenship and deferred action under DACA may be terminated at any time, with or without a Notice of Intent to Terminate, at DHS's discretion.

The millions of children already covered under DACA have also faced the risk of being deported at any time.

One such teenager was Oscar Vasquez whose story and circumstances were highlighted in the movie, Spare Parts, starring George Lopez and Marisa Tomei. Oscar came to the U.S. when he was very young. He wanted to go into the U.S. Army legally but couldn't do so because of his undocumented status. Many such kids age out of any protection programs when they no longer qualify as a dependent. In Oscar's case, he self-deported to Mexico, where he lived and worked for several months. It was only after the intervention of U.S. Senator Dick Durbin that Oscar was allowed back into the United States. He enlisted in the U.S. Army and served in Afghanistan. Upon his return, Oscar was finally able to become a United States citizen.

People living in Latin America have heard story after story of mothers, fathers and children being deported to countries where they have not lived possibly for most or all their life. These separated parents are willing to remain this way so their children can have a chance at a better, brighter future than the one they faced in their country. No government website is going to dispel these fears or take the place of ongoing efforts to locate parents and get them to provide contact information with the hope that the U.S. government will make substantial restitution for these horrible family separations.

Chapter Eight

Separation and Incarceration Stories from the Border

Nothing brings a point home like reading a story from someone who has lived through an event unless HBO makes a movie about it. Our work doesn't often put us in direct contact with those parents who were separated from their children. Fortunately, we have received some personal accounts from a few other families. Their comments may help to paint a better picture of what has happened to thousands of families.

I have kept the stories as intact as possible and have only added some information in brackets [ ] to help clarify a thought. Otherwise, what you will read below are the words as we received them.

A family from Huehuetenango in Guatemala passed their story to us.

> *I wanted to go to the United States with my daughter. I arrived safely, and my daughter also arrived safely with me. When I got to the Mexico-U.S. border, they*

wouldn't let me leave with my daughter. They only gave me a chance to be with her for 24 hours, then they separated us, and I didn't see her anymore.

She called me at the jail about a week or more after that happened. She felt it was good when we were able to talk. She told me she was fine. I didn't know where my daughter was or how much food they gave her, but she told me she was getting whatever she wanted. She would go out to play. She could be with other children. They were given a half hour [a day]. She felt good with the people she was with during that time; she felt they treated her well. She was never hurt, and she didn't see anyone get hurt either. My daughter was separated [and in U.S. federal care] for about a month and a half before she was placed with a relative.

They [officers] didn't say anything to me. They let me talk to my family in Guatemala. They treated me well, but they gave me very little food. We would get food at 6am and then nothing until 8pm. Some of the men would faint. The Hondurans and Brazilians almost died. It wasn't fair the amount of food they gave us. I became very thin during that month. It was a hard experience. I was in three prisons, Hidalgo, then I went to Texas and then to Sierra Blanca. Then they deported me back to Guatemala by plane. I had a little money because my sister sent me 50 or 100 dollars. That is why I had money when I came back.

I came straight to Guatemala. When I arrived, I got on a gray bus that brought me to Huehuetenango. I paid my transportation in Huehue to get to my house because I live farther away from Huehue, but no one offered me more help.

Now my daughter is studying and doing well. She already speaks English. Now she doesn't want to speak our dialect anymore. She speaks it but only two or five words of our dialect. She almost only wants to speak English. We speak Akateko so it is a little difficult to talk to her.

I want to go with my son [back to the U.S.]. I heard that President Donald Trump said that migrants with their children could enter again. I wanted to go back, but I don't have the money to go with my son, so I didn't go again.

*   *   *

This story was passed to us from a father from Honduras.

A mother and her two children came from Honduras to the U.S. border. Three or four days after the mother and her kids were stopped at the border, the kids were not only separated from the mother but were separated from each other for a time. The mother had her children's birth certificates and her own identification from Honduras. She saw a lot of people with children that were not theirs when she was crossing, and they were not separated as this mother and her kids had been. It seemed that it was a lot easier to cross the border with children so many people take other children with them. Yet in this case it did not go well for this mother and her kids.

Immigration [officials] told her that the kids were going to be in a better place. They were taken to

an immigration center, and their mother was sanc-
tioned with a felony as she had illegally crossed
the border. The mother reported to her husband
that she and the kids had been separated. At the
time the mother was placed in federal custody, she
also had 3,000 Mexico pesos, about US $147.

The father located an immigration phone number
and asked about his children. They [officials] asked
why he was looking for these children. They asked
a lot of questions. In contrast, his wife had said
that officials didn't ask her a lot of questions. The
father knew he could get deported, but he needed
to find his children. Immigration services informed
him that in El Paso all shelters were full, so his two
kids had been sent to New York.

The representative mentioned that the children
had been separated. The father asked the social
worker if his kids could be placed together again.
A week later the father received information that
the kids were back together. He was able to get
the phone number where they were located and
was able to call them. They said they used to cry,
and they were upset as they were scared more
so when they were separated. The father called
them to make sure that they were calm. The social
worker passed along information that it had been
very difficult for the kids. It was chaos with too
many children and that the situation was too
complicated.

His kids were still under the care of Immigration
even though they had been sent to New York. To
the best of this father's knowledge, no organization

helped him. He did not know of anyone else who could help him.

It was this social worker who helped the father out. The father said he got lucky because he got a Hispanic social worker that spoke Spanish. The social worker was also the guardian for several unaccompanied minors from his own family that had crossed the border. This official had had some experience in the past with Immigration, so he knew a bit about the process.

[Just because someone works for U.S. Immigration doesn't mean they automatically know all the processes about working with children separated from their parents. Until "zero tolerance" was initiated, the vast majority of families stayed together so this separation process was new.]

The father wrote that his two kids were scared. They were scared because no one explained anything to them. They said they used to cry, and they were very upset as they were scared more so when they were separated. The kids told their father that there was scarce food. They did get milk. Yet it was not great accommodations. There were lots of children. They were in a shelter. They did not have actual beds, but more like cots. The kids told their father several times that they did not sleep much. They would wake up in the middle of the night because they became afraid and scared and alone or due to some kids crying. The kids told their father that the people were not the friendliest. There were so many kids together that if one began crying this would prompt others to become scared.

The father remembered his kids telling him that the social workers were not very patient as they had to deal with so many children. His kids were placed in areas where they could not leave or do much. They had to be as quiet as possible and cause as little trouble because the people were not the nicest. The father does not remember much and neither do his children as it was over three years ago. He did say that his kids were infested with lice when he got them, but other than that, they did not have any other evidence of being harmed.

The kids stayed in a shelter [federal facility] during the entire time their father was petitioning for custody. It took almost two months to get custody of his kids.

The kids' mother was incarcerated for six months in El Paso. No one in the U.S. asked her any questions or requested any information from her. The place where she was incarcerated was full of immigrants. She was only with women. She was not treated very well. There were too many women. The treatment overall was very poor.

The day she was released, the mother was chained up and sent back to Honduras in a plane with other people who were being deported. U.S. Immigration never did return her ID card nor her money once she was released from the El Paso facility. The only reason the mother was deported back to Honduras was because Immigration staff had taken her ID and knew that she was from Honduras.

*   *   *

This story is about a father and his teenage son.

During their trip from Mexico they had to hide in buses. Organized crime in Mexico specifically looks for migrant buses to rob and they had to give up everything they had to avoid losing their lives. At the U.S. border, the coyotes were the ones who tried to guide them on the safest route, but the police still caught them.

They were taken to the cold room the same night they arrived so they didn't have to wait many hours, but they were handcuffed from the moment they arrived. In the cold room they were already separated from their children, who were all about sixteen years old. As far as the father knows, the children were also handcuffed and all their belongings were taken away.

Regarding the cold room and the food they were given, the father said: "They put us in there because they wanted us to suffer so we wouldn't come back" because it was so cold and they [the parents] had no place to sleep or anything to keep warm, just a piece of aluminum that did not keep them warm. The same treatment for the children.

About the food, they [officers] only gave them 1 cookie each and a juice. He said that the cookie was like ones they sell in Guatemala for Q0.50 and a juice for about Q2.00, very bad quality.

*   *   *

Another parent talked about his family's experience.

The father traveled with his daughter who was four years old and his wife. At the border with Mexico, they [the coyotes] put them on buses. "With the authorities there and the organized crime you have to hide." They had to go around Mexico, with boats, trains and everything. It was a difficult journey. On that trip they were robbed of more than 60,000 Mexican pesos [about US$3,000]. The people in charge of them were very irresponsible. They were drunk most of the time and hardly gave them any food during the trip. When the families arrived in the United States, they were told [by the coyotes] that they had to turn themselves in to Immigration and that is when they separated the father and his daughter. The father's wife and his daughter were taken to another bus, and he never heard from them again. He saw how his wife was handcuffed. They also handcuffed him and only gave him a loaf of bread and a bottle of water.

Upon arrival, they handcuffed the father and tied him up in the cold room without anything to keep him warm. "It was with the intention of making us suffer that they put us in there. They did not give me food for three days until they moved me to jail." The officers gave the father enough food, but they treated him very badly. He felt that the officers were going to kick him or beat him at any moment, and they told the father repeatedly that he only wanted to enter the United States because he wanted to steal.

He spent 25 days in detention and all the way back to Guatemala he was handcuffed. "They [U.S. officers] treat us the same or worse than a criminal." When the father arrived, there was no organization to support him. As he had no money, he spent two days in the capital trying to find someone to lend him money so he could return home.

*   *   *

Finally, one last story that another parent shared about his and his daughter's experience.

This father said that he and his eight-year-old daughter were treated well by the coyotes, but that in the United States they were separated immediately. They only gave him a package of cookies for food and put him in a cold room, handcuffed and without anything to keep him warm. He says they treated him as if he were a criminal when he was just trying to make a better life for his family. He was detained for five months until he was returned to El Salvador. During this time the treatment was not good, but they gave him enough food, although not like he was used to eating in El Salvador. On the way back, he was also handcuffed on the plane, without permission to go to the bathroom. When he arrived in El Salvador, there was no organization or group to support him to return home.

About his daughter, the father said that she was not handcuffed because she was very young, but they were separated immediately. They [officers] did not let them talk for all those months. She was in a shelter where they treated her well. However, she was also deported after six or seven months and is now with her family.

*   *   *

After reading these stories, your feelings may range from sympathy to apathy. We can only hope that whatever trauma these parents and children suffered while asking for asylum in the U.S. will diminish with time.

While the U.S. government says it's working toward reunification, some children as young as eight-years-old have been deported. Then how serious is the government?! Either it has lost control and doesn't know whom it's deporting, or the government has no true intention of reuniting families. If this is what politicians and the government believe are *"Christian family values,"* then turn off the sound because the hypocrisy is deafening. Instead, the U.S. government needs to make good on that executive order to reunite parents once again with their children.

Chapter Nine

Barriers to Latino Foster Kids' Reunification Success

The U.S. government has no idea where more than a thousand children are. These children could easily be on the street, and some of these children are now ending up in the U.S. foster care system. However, since the federal system and the foster care system don't talk to each other, the federal government has no way of knowing that many children separated from their parents are now in foster or group homes.

Let's talk for a moment about how an immigrant child can move from federal care, be placed with a sponsor, and end up in U.S. foster care. As mentioned before, the children who were separated from their parent at the Mexico-U.S. border went into federal care under the ORR. The agency is charged with identifying appropriate sponsors living in the U.S. who can care for the child when he or she leaves ORR custody. Many kids were processed within a few weeks to two months and placed with a sponsor, but there is no official timeline as to how quickly a child must be placed with a sponsor. Where no appropriate sponsors are found, children remain in ORR custody and may be placed in long-term foster care, including community-based foster care or a group home. It's important to point out that ORR is not a law enforcement agency and has no role in the decision to separate families or prosecute immigration law violations.

Sometimes a child gets stuck in the system even when ORR is aware of an appropriate sponsor. Molly Chew, Project Director for the nonprofit VECINA, shared that ORR sets a high priority on placing a child with a sponsor who is their parent. In cases where a child's anticipated sponsor may be a distant relative, those cases have a much lower priority.

These sponsors may require more vetting to ensure they will be an appropriate placement for the child. For these cases, VECINA works on behalf of the child and family to help expedite the release of the child to their sponsor. These adults often have difficulty understanding the documents they received from ORR and may be incapable of providing the needed information so that the child can be released to them. VECINA has experienced staff and works with other organizations who then work with these sponsors whether it's in Spanish or in an Indigenous language such as K'iche' or Sakapultek. The result is that a child is often placed more quickly with a sponsor.

Only about 25 percent of the kids who are placed with a sponsor receive ongoing monitoring by ORR or a contracted service provider. These kids who are considered to be in "post release custody" are monitored and may receive services up to 90 days. The other kids in this group will remain under ORR care until they turn 18 because a sponsor wasn't found. Of the remaining 75 percent of the kids who are released to a sponsor, they only receive a follow up call thirty days later. After that call, the child is considered released by ORR. The child is now living with their sponsor and will go on with their life until their case comes up for judicial review to resolve their immigration status.

During this time waiting for a judicial review is when contact can easily be lost with the child and/or their sponsor. An immigrant child is also in a home situation where they may be placed in state or county foster care. Kids enter foster care because of abuse, neglect or criminal activity by their parent or guardian. Virtually every immigrant child is going to a low-income home. The child's sponsor may be in the U.S. without proper documents meaning that the adult is usually forced to accept low paying jobs that pay cash and provide no health care or job benefits. Families may have to move due to rent increases and lack of income. You can now see how the federal government lost track of thousands of separated children.

Whether a child is U.S.-born or an immigrant, once they are in foster care, agencies are supposed to treat them as any other child meaning they start the family finding process. Keep in mind that whatever problems the U.S. federal government has been experiencing with trying to locate separated parents, state and county foster care agencies will have those similar challenges starting with needing caseworkers who knows how to speak, read, understand, and communicate in Spanish. This may seem like a no-brainer, but one of the problems has been that agencies have either limited or no staff who speak Spanish.

Years ago, only a few states along the border had large populations of Latinos such as Arizona, California, Florida and Texas. Now Latinos are in all parts of the United States. The state of Illinois has one of the largest Latino populations in the country. Foster care agencies that previously didn't have Spanish-speaking staff now need them along with the legally required paperwork in Spanish. Many foster care agencies are having to set up a whole new process for Latino children and their families. I mentioned previously about a grand jury's findings listing 36 violations that the Napa County in California had committed on its foster children.

> One of the most critical findings was that the county's services to Latinos was: *"made more difficult due to the high percentage of children and parents who are Spanish speaking... and three foster homes out of 40-45 include bilingual parents."*

However, it's not just California counties. Illinois' failings were highlighted in the 2019 ProPublica article which quoted State Sen. Julie Morrison saying,

> *"How in 2019 do we not have enough Spanish-speaking caseworkers? If it was Mandarin, I'd say that is tough. But there is no excuse for this."*

Even if a foster care agency has a caseworker who speaks Spanish, this doesn't guarantee that there will not be challenges communicating with either the child or their relatives. Native Spanish speakers sometimes struggle to understand what someone in another Latino country is saying. Imagine this scenario with someone who's working in the foster care system. The agency may have a staff member who took two years of college Spanish, and they're trying to talk to someone in some Central or South American country who speaks with an accent. That can be a difficult conversation for both people. This is the same challenge that people in the United States have when listening to someone from England or from Louisiana who has a Creole accent. People speak differently depending upon which part of the world they are from even if both are speaking Spanish or English.

Unfortunately, foster care agencies are starting to have even more challenges when working with Latino kids. Agencies no longer have just the concern of having staff who speak Spanish. More kids who are entering the foster care system are coming from regions in Central America where the dominant language is not Spanish. Some of their families are from parts of Guatemala where they only speak an Indigenous language such as Acateco or K'iche'.

Even if a foster care agency has someone who speaks Spanish, there are familiar problems that can make a family finding effort unsuccessful starting with collecting information to use to locate relatives. We worked a case where one of the last names was spelled Zotelo. This was the way that the name was spelled on the birth certificate. However, Zotelo is a rare spelling for a last name in Spanish. Sotelo is much more common. This name could easily have been misspelled because "s" sounds like "z" in Spanish. Sotelo sounds like it should be spelled Zotelo in English. If a foster care caseworker or a Border Patrol official heard this name, it's very easy to understand how a misspelling could happen. We located the foster child's relatives because our specialist did a new search using the spelling Sotelo.

Misspellings with the names of states and cities can make it impossible to locate a child's relatives. A young Latino man in the U.S. was trying to find his sister in Mexico. He wrote that his sister lived in the Mexican state of "Cuahuila." There is no state with that spelling. It's actually Coahuila, but this Latino man maintained that he had spelled the name properly. Fortunately, we made the correction and located his sister.

Another example: There are a set of towns in an area of Guatemala. Let's say that a caseworker received a report to locate a relative, and the city was spelled Amacchel. Unfortunately, no town is named Amacchel, and because of the age of the child, there would be no way to verify the spelling. Here are all the possibilities that the foster care agency could be facing: Antiguo Ajmachel, Los Encuentros Ajmachel, Xecol Amajchel, Nuevo Amajchel, La Esperanza Amajchel, Vella Vista Amajchel and Ajmachel Centro.

Every county that has Latino foster kids faces these same obstacles. These agencies need someone who has the expertise to know that the information it is receiving is incorrect. One of the biggest benefits that Forever Homes provides to foster care agencies is an analysis of the information they provide us. We often have to go back to the intake person or caseworker and ask them to re-interview the child or the parents because some information is inaccurate or not good.

When children, including immigrant kids, come into the foster care system, they're usually coming in because of an issue with a parent or guardian. If the caseworker is interviewing the parents, they may not provide truthful information. Other times they may hold back information for whatever reason. A caseworker may take the information exactly how it was given to them and did an outstanding job of writing it down. Yet for whatever reason, a parent or relative may give incorrect information.

If the person interviewed was a child, they may be of an age that they simply don't have any information to provide to government agencies or nonprofits. They also may not have much education, so they simply have no idea where they lived. Parents often sew address tags onto their kids' clothing in the United States because their children are too young to remember where they live.

I had a situation like this when I was young. I was probably six years old and had gone out on Halloween trick-or-treating with two of my neighbors, one who was a couple of years older. We were supposed to stick together, but at one point I raced to the next house and rang the doorbell.

After getting my candy, I turned around and didn't see my neighbors behind me. I looked around some more and couldn't find either of them. To this day I have no idea if they decided to hide or what they decided to do, but at that moment I realized that I was lost. I wandered around for what seemed like a long time. Finally, I ran into an old couple. They were very nice. They asked me where I lived, but I couldn't tell them. I didn't remember the name of the street. I knew what the houses looked like. I knew a few other landmarks, but I was not able to tell them the name of the street. They walked around with me for probably half an hour until I finally got close to my street, and then I knew where I was.

I had lived in the same home for four years so you might imagine that at six years old I probably knew where I was living. But I didn't at least not at nighttime. Now imagine a child who has not only left their neighborhood but also left their country. They've gone through another country or two, and now they're at a place where people speak a completely different language. They're just not able to be very helpful with finding their relatives.

You may be thinking, *"This sounds hopeless."* The prospect of doing family finding internationally in Latin America may sound like it's next to impossible, but it's not. Right now, parents and relatives are being located even with minimal information. Children are being reunited with their families. In the movie, *For Love or Money*, Michael J. Fox says this amazing line, *"Nothing is impossible. Impossible just takes a couple of extra phone calls."* Every kid in foster care deserves that same attitude and commitment.

We worked a case years ago involving three sisters, ages four, eight and ten. These children had all been born and lived in the United States. They all spoke English. When the caseworker came to Forever Homes, the girls had only been able to give limited information about their relatives living in Mexico and that two aunts were living in Chicago. No names for the aunts, no addresses, no telephone numbers.

In a matter of weeks, we located an uncle and aunt living in Mexico. This case ended up having an amazing ending. On a Saturday, the caseworker had someone who spoke Spanish with her. They called to Mexico and ended up speaking with an uncle. After a few minutes of explaining who the caseworker was and why she was calling, she asked him if he knew about the two aunts living in Chicago. He told the caseworker to wait a moment. Several seconds later a woman came on the line. The caseworker once again introduced herself and explained why she was calling and asked the woman if she happened to know anything about these two aunts living in Chicago, to which the woman said, *"Yes, I'm one of the aunts."*

The two aunts had flown to Mexico and were spending the week with the uncle and his family. Everyone had been sitting in the living room when the caseworker called. The caseworker was absolutely blown away. It was so exciting listening to her excitement when she explained what had happened and about that moment of discovery involving one of the aunts. As you may imagine, the girls left foster care and went to live in Chicago.

Family finding works. The road to successful reunification is not without difficulties, but every effort needs to be made by foster care agencies so that all children are afforded the care they deserve.

Chapter Ten

Aging Out, Forced Expulsion of Foster Kids

For 17-year-old teenagers who live with their family, their thoughts are mainly focused on their future and going to college or a trade school. In contrast, foster kids of the same age in almost half of the states are thinking about where they'll be sleeping or getting their next meal once they turn 18. These kids are usually scared because instead of a birthday cake and presents, they will lose their home, their friends and whatever sense of security they have because they will be forced out of the foster care system.

Moving out of the home may happen in the morning or maybe in the afternoon when they return home from school. But sometime during the day, each teen will have to clean out their closet or drawer. Some may have a suitcase; many others will have to use a trash bag. Someone from CPS will come by, pick them up and drop them off someplace, maybe at a hotel or shelter unless the teen has made arrangements to stay with someone. Some may have less than $50 in cash on them provided by CPS. This money has to pay for food and a place to sleep and hopefully secure their belongings. Happy Birthday.

One former foster kid from Austin, Texas shared a little about the day when she aged out and her experience. Tania said that her foster mom offered to let her continue to stay in the home, but she decided to leave anyway. Tania just grabbed a trash bag to put her things in and left. She didn't have any money. She was able to couch surf for a while and then moved to San Antonio, Texas. She was homeless for about two years until she reached out to her ILS (Independent Living Skills) caseworker who was able to get Tania into a shelter. She has been working at the same company for a few years now. Tania shared that many former foster kids don't want to talk about their experiences because doing so can bring back very painful memories. Former foster kids may still be struggling with homelessness, the inability to get and keep a job or other issues that were never properly addressed while they were in foster care.

Depending upon the city and state, as much as 30% of foster children who age out have not finished high school. That's roughly 6,900 students each year. In their article, "States Tackle 'Aging Out' of Foster Care," the Pew Charitable Trusts revealed even worse numbers. *"Fifty-eight percent of foster youth will graduate high school by age 19, compared to 87 percent of all 19-year-olds."*

Either way, this means that not only do these children need to find a place to live and sleep, now they need a place to keep their books and a place to study. All this can be especially challenging when that child has no income and is spending the bulk of their time trying to find food and a safe place to sleep.

A caseworker shared a very sad story. She had a 17-year-old foster teen who knew that he would be aging out within the next seven months. He told his caseworker that he felt his only possible path was to turn to prostitution. He didn't want to do this, but he did not see himself being able to get and hold down a job and earn enough money that would allow him to eat and have a place to stay.

For children who age out, homelessness is one of the severe challenges they will experience. An Oklahoma City Times Record article by Sidney Lee shouted, "Oklahoma DHS: 30 Percent of Foster Care Youth Who Age Out Experience Homelessness."

Connie Schlittler, director of the Office of Planning, Research and Statistics for the Oklahoma Department of Human Services said:

> *"We have an obligation to do better by children who are in child welfare custody."* She continued to condemn the system as *"a pipeline for homelessness,"* that adds thousands of foster teens to the ranks of the homeless each year.

A few years ago in San Diego, there was an outbreak of hepatitis A. This breakout was so severe that the city had to come in and power wash the sidewalks to remove the urine and feces and clean up the area where the homeless were staying. Many former foster kids live in such an environment. Some truly have no place to turn to, no shelter to stay at and are forced to sleep outside at great risk.

Many cities have policies in place so that the police will actively stop homeless people from eating food they have received from well-meaning donors. Stories abound where the police have harassed or even arrested the volunteers themselves who gave food to these homeless people. Some government officials are pushing even harsher treatment that will affect homeless foster kids. Tennessee Gov. Bill Lee is preparing to sign Senate Bill 1610/House Bill 0978 into law this week to criminalize homelessness. The Nashville Tennessean article explains that the law would *"make camping on all public property across the state a class E felony."* As an aside – entering the U.S. without documents is only a misdemeanor.

A June 2016 article by the Seattle Weekly brings home how poorly the foster care system is managed when it comes to tackling homelessness:

> *"The foster care system doesn't even collect data on kids who become homeless in the system; only by interviewing teens who are living on the streets and in shelters did the Children and Families Administration arrive at its figures of homeless teens with a history in foster care. In essence, homeless youth in the child welfare system don't exist on paper."*

Thousands of kids choose to leave their foster home because they feel the streets provide the "lesser of two evils" – a way out of an environment where they know they will continue to be physically, emotionally, or sexually abused. These kids often choose to run away from their foster home situation rather than remain victimized, which, in turn, puts them at high risk of being attacked, raped, or killed on the streets. Thousands of children enter the foster care system because of physical and sexual abuse. Unfortunately, nearly one in three children is abused while in foster care and not always by an adult. One such example is the story about a young man who is known to have abused other foster boys when he was in foster homes. Instead of being separated and having children protected from him, caseworkers continued to place him in foster homes and did not let the foster parents know that he had a history of sexually molesting boys.

One former foster kid said that she had run away and that her boyfriend/pimp would "beat her ass" but that this was preferable to her being in foster care. Adding to those cases where foster children are forced to run away for their own safety, there is the growing crisis of sex traffickers who aggressively go after foster youths.

In late 2014, the FBI conducted its largest national sex trafficking raid, one that spanned the country. In the aftermath of multiple raids, documents showed that many children who were forced into prostitution and sold as sex slaves had been in the welfare system, including foster care.

A Los Angeles Times article highlighted this issue, saying that the raids: *"brought renewed attention to the vulnerabilities of foster children, who are disproportionately targeted and recruited by child sex traffickers, sometimes right out of the foster care system."*

When faced with homelessness and no financial or family support, one can only imagine how much more appealing life could seem to a foster teen when at least offered food and a place to live – even if ultimately the teen will be forced into sex and committing crimes in order to stay alive.

Law enforcement and sex trafficking experts have shared that a child who ages out of foster care can get caught up in sex trafficking in as little as six hours from the time they age out. The drop off spots for newly aged out children is known to sex traffickers just as it is known to community leaders. During a Senate Finance Committee meeting, one of the senators commented how in his district there were plans for a shelter for homeless people. The location was chosen in part because it was down the street from the known drop off site for foster children. The idea was that if these kids knew the shelter was there, they would find their way to it so that they could get food and have a safe place to sleep.

Not every foster kid is lucky enough to be dropped off at a location close to a homeless shelter. Antwone Fisher, the guest speaker at the same Senate Finance Committee meeting, shared that he was taken to a hotel in the center of town and given only $60. However, as Antwone was checking in, the front desk clerk warned him not to go above the second floor because men were raping boys there. There's nothing more reassuring than knowing that a county agency is dropping off foster teens at a building that has floors full of rapists, pimps and prostitutes.

All of these outcomes that happen to roughly 80% of foster children are based on an exhaustive study by the National Coalition for Child Protection Reform. These same sad outcomes will probably happen to immigrant children who are placed in foster care. Except in their case, these immigrant children may have few relatives in the United States, or there may be few to no relatives that they are aware of and that they will never find without the aid of professionals who have the resources and expertise to help.

Amplifying the use of family finding would result in more foster kids being placed with relatives. Caseworkers would be able to give more attention to the decreased number of children under their care. Funds could be shifted to ensure that each child receives the physical and psychological therapies that they need. Relatives who take in a foster child could be paid more than, in some cases, $75 a month per child. This amount, presently the stipend that relatives received in Arizona, is barely enough to feed one teenager for one week.

Many teens who thought they could go it alone without any family connections explained how reality had set in. They recognized too late how much they needed a family safety net. For thousands of foster children, once they age out, it's difficult, if not impossible, for them to locate distant relatives on their own.

> *"I thought I knew everything when I decided to age out [of foster care] at 18 without family relationships,"* says Natalia Gomez from Portland, Oregon. *"But then I realized I didn't."*

> Said Monse Richardson of Alvin, Texas, *"The most important thing I want caseworkers to know is that every teen needs that chance for a forever family."*

Recent changes and proposals in some states allow kids to stay in the foster care system longer than age 18 to help them finish high school and/or get into college. Even so, foster kids still face many financial challenges such as needing money or landing a job to afford food, a room or apartment, clothes and transportation. This lack of income for thousands of youths has led to a growing focus by federal and state agencies on ways to help these foster kids once they leave the system. A handful of states are establishing programs designed to help former foster kids until they turn 25. Additionally, more nonprofits are springing up or expanding their existing programs to encompass these aged-out children.

Over the last ten years transitional programs have been developed to help youths who age out. These programs will always be necessary for a small percentage of foster teens. ABC had a segment titled, "Aging Out, But Not Abandoned; Program Helps Foster Kids Stay on Track."

Transitional housing is an important piece of the overall strategy to help foster kids become self-sustaining. Some transitional programs include a core focus on getting foster teenagers into colleges. While as students, foster youths enjoy food and housing during the school semester, many find themselves homeless, couch surfing or living in a car during semester breaks.

However, the creation of transitional programs does not come without its own problems, and the programs are costly. Even with plentiful housing, which is often not the case, former foster youths often have to contend with landlords who may see these potential tenants as delinquents and troublemakers. While many teenagers have a parent or relative to cosign for an apartment, reducing a landlord's concern about possible monetary loss, most foster teenagers have no such financial support.

The Pew Charitable Trusts article mentioned previously sums up a glaring problem with transitional programs.

> *"You almost need to build a second foster care system,"* said Hope Cooper, a consultant who worked on the federal legislation effort. *"This is a system that has*

to serve kids that are pregnant, kids that want to live alone, and they have to voluntarily join (or stay in) foster care. It's almost a parallel foster care system."

Another serious problem is with communication. While transitional programs are run by foster care agencies and nonprofits, many foster children find it challenging to learn about these programs or get through the paperwork on their own without the help of an adult.

In an article by News 4 San Antonio reporter Emily Baucum, former foster child turned advocate, Krizia Ramirez Franklin, said:

"In working with teenagers who are aging out of foster care, I hear all the time: 'I asked my caseworker about my Tuition & Fee Waiver, she had no idea what it was, he had no idea. I asked them about Transitional Living Services, they had no idea what I was talking about, they told me that we didn't have any of those services here in San Antonio.' Things like that. Those are things that every case manager should know."

By the time many children in foster care reach age 18, even if there are transitional programs available, they may be so fed up with the foster care system that they are willing to leave despite the help that is available for them.

More needs to be done to protect and safeguard foster children, so they don't fall through the cracks or run away.

Our obligation as a society to care for foster kids includes ensuring they have a safe home environment, and that their medical and emotional needs are being properly addressed.

Part of this care includes preventing an environment of abuse in which youths leave a home only to become another member of the homeless or, worse, a victim of sex trafficking.

There is no one-size-fits-all, and agencies need to look at solutions both while a child is in the foster care system and once they are forced to be on their own. Although there will always be the need to have some form of group home, if foster care agencies would provide good family finding services to children while they are still in foster care, thousands of foster children could be placed with family and out of the foster care system.

Performing more family finding will certainly work to benefit thousands of foster children who would now have the potential to be connected with relatives. When these foster kids age out, they can choose to live with their aunts, uncles and other relatives or at least have that vital family connection that many non-foster youths take for granted. No matter how it happens, keeping foster children from becoming homeless is a critical priority for foster care agencies.

At the end of the day this comment from a colleague of Connie Schlittler at the Oklahoma Department of Human Services sums up the foster child homeless crisis:

> *"It's wrong that we take kids away from their families and the state of Oklahoma says we're going to take care of them, and this is the outcome: that they become homeless."*

Chapter Eleven

Foster Care System's Dangers and Abuses

I got blindsided by two instances of abuse in my personal world. One came from my niece and the other from the sister of a friend. Both cases gave me a painful reminder of how our children are being abused while in U.S. foster care.

My niece's experience stems from a pervasive problem in the workplace. She works in the sciences industry. When she started working with one company, her male supervisor was pleasant. As some point, he asked my niece out. She politely said no. He immediately became hostile, yelling at her at times and making her work environment very uncomfortable. My niece was 25 years old, but she wasn't prepared to handle this type of workplace abuse.

She ended up leaving the company.

How does that tie into the abuses that foster children suffer? Here's how:

All too often adults treat children, especially foster children, like little adults. They aren't. They are children who look up to adults in general for guidance and protection. Children also have this endearing yet frightening trust in almost everyone. This makes kids vulnerable to abuse. They may believe that abusive behavior, including sexual abuse, is normal. They may sense that something isn't quite right, but because they can't articulate these thoughts, children will often hide them.

I don't know with whom my niece talked about her situation. It certainly wasn't common knowledge within the family until months after she had quit. My niece had graduated from college and has traveled to other countries. She's sharp and educated, yet she is just now coming to grips with her abuse.

Now imagine a foster child who is being abused. How likely is it that they will tell someone? If the abuse is happening in the home, the child may not tell the other parent for many reasons, not the least being their fear that they may receive more abuse. Children aren't stupid. They may not be able to speak about their fears and abuse, but they know the possible results. They know what sets off a parent or relative.

Unfortunately, we still have too many laws that limit when a child can come forward to talk about their abuse and find some justice. A 2016 Next Avenue article revealed that many people only start to share about their abuse decades later. The "Adverse Childhood Experiences" or ACE Study states:

> *"data found that childhood sexual abuse was reported by just 16 percent of males and 25 percent of females. Men who were sexually abused as kids waited an average of 21 years before they told a single person about the abuse. It took them 28 years to give a fuller account to someone else."*

One state has a law where the victim is given just two years from the time of the abuse to come forward and make a formal complaint.

Jane E. Palmer, a professorial lecturer at the Department of Justice, Law & Criminology at American University School of Public Affairs, covered state laws from several states in an article in "The Conversation" with the headline, "New Laws Give Victims More Time to Report Rape or Sexual Assault – Even Jeffrey Epstein's." The Child Victims Act in New York now gives abuse victims until age 28 to report a childhood assault. The law *"also allows more time for victims to sue alleged perpetrators or negligent institutions – until age 55."*

Palmer highlighted that, as of the summer of 2019, eight states have no restrictions on the time when an abuse victim can step forward. Again, this acknowledges in part the reality that many, if not most, abuse victims do not step forward until they are in their 40s or 50s.

The other incident of abuse came from the sister of a good friend of mine.

Susan had been miserable at her job for years. Family, friends and even her physicians had listened to her complaints about how unhappy she was at her job. Sadly, a necessary step for some victims is to finally become so unsatisfied, frustrated and/or discontented with their feelings that they start looking for ways to get rid of them.

No one wants to see family members and friends suffering. It's not that others and I didn't try to talk to Susan about her situation. We did, but a victim probably has to be on board with the idea that they are a victim. All too often victims will look for bright spots, saying things like, *"Well, this week my boss didn't yell at me."* or *"Sometimes she can be a nice person."*

You have probably heard about the Stockholm Syndrome, where a prisoner will end up identifying with their jailer/abuser. Mental health professionals used to relate this psychological trauma just to hostage situations. However, over the years, psychiatrists have expanded the effects of this trauma to include many more situations involving abused children, incest victims and workplace incidents. A common denominator is relationships that are controlling or intimidating. A feeling of being trapped can trigger this syndrome. It can occur at home, school or workplaces where a person may feel obligated to remain despite their fears or urge to flee.

The situation can involve a child who is beholden to an abusive parent, foster parent or teacher. It can involve a worker who feels trapped because the pay allows them to feel just comfortable enough not to be dissatisfied with their work environment despite years of verbal, emotional or sexual harassment.

Susan was fortunate that she took a harassment training course online. Her moment of awakening was when the program displayed a checklist of abusive behavior. Susan started slowing reading the list on the monitor. One by one, she started to say to herself, *"That's happened here. They've insulted me about my clothes. They've criticized me about how I wear my hair."* She kept going down this long list and realized that she had been abused in almost every way. She started to cry. She liked her boss. She liked the job more or less, but now she knew that she had been seriously abused for years. She wanted to shut off the computer and leave, but she stayed and finished the course. For the first time, she knew that the information was coming from a verified source and could see all of the issues she had been experiencing for years laid out before her. Susan finally realized that she had been and still was being abused. Saddened, Susan sat up, grabbed some tissue, blew her nose and wiped away the tear. She now knew that she had to quit and get out of that toxic environment.

Susan quit her job within a week. She considered legal action, but she just wanted to get away. Foster children rarely feel so confident to talk about their abuses and so are unable to fight back. The result? Nearly a third of foster children are abused while in the system, and those are just the ones we know about.

One of the ways that foster child abuse flourishes in the system is that abusers can take advantage of the nomadic life of foster children. These children move an average of twice a year. Some have reported being moved more than five times during a year. This movement can allow a child to leave a safe haven such as a school where they felt trusting enough to tell a teacher about an abuse, or where school officials could detect that some form of abuse had taken place. Abusers count on the natural fear and/or trust children have toward an adult and this constant movement to hide an adult's abusive ways.

Most, if not all, professions have a creed and an idealized version that people in these professions strive to achieve. For doctors it's *"Do no harm."* Police are sworn *"To protect and to serve."* In the foster care system, adults join the ranks of volunteers who are willing to become foster parents and give a foster child the care, love and stability they so desperately need. In every category there are those adults who do a good, even an outstanding job. Yet some not only fall far short of their mission but become the exact opposite – an abuser, attacker and/or murderer.

Let's put into perspective the critical nature of this abuse that occurs once a child is in foster care. The Annie E. Casey Foundation reports that about 18% of foster kids are removed from their parent(s) due to physical or sexual abuse. By placing a child into foster care, the risk of that child being abused almost doubles compared to leaving them with their parents in the first place. More than 40,800 children who were never abused at home are now likely to be abused while in foster care.

The disturbing reality is that despite the thousands of caring adults who become foster parents for all the right reasons, fewer but still thousands of others are sexual predators and abusers, twisted people who have no problem with hurting little children.

The December 2021 Dayton Daily News article, "Mother Sues Montgomery County, Children Services Employees After Child Sexually Abused," uncovered that the woman's daughter [and brother while in foster care] had been placed with Teaven Curtiss. He *"had been accused of multiple sex crimes dating back to 2006,"* and that *"children services employees knew about Curtiss' past criminal issues before placing the children with him. Curtiss was charged and convicted in 2020 of raping the 4-year-old girl and was sentenced to prison for life without parole."*

The article ends with these comments from Montgomery County Prosecutor Mat Heck Jr.: *"If those responsible would have heeded the red flags present, the abuse this child suffered may never have happened. This is another tragic child abuse case, showing that we must be vigilant, and continue to put in extra care and effort, which anyone involved in these types of cases should expect. Children deserve no less."*

Tragically, the consequences of abuse can also have fatal outcomes.

Natalie Finn was just 16 when she died on the floor of her unfurnished bedroom. A Des Moines Register article, "Starved Teen Found in Diaper on Linoleum Floor, Records Reveal," said that the cause of death was attributed to emaciation. Natalie was so starved that her body simply lacked the strength to keep her heart beating. Starvation is a slow and painful process that no one, especially a child, should have to endure.

Natalie's abusers were her two adoptive parents, Nicole Finn and ex-husband Joe Finn. Police who found Natalie shared that there was plenty of food in the house. The girl had attended school but was being home-schooled at the time of her death. Joe revealed that he had nailed the window shut in the bedroom of Natalie and her two siblings so they couldn't go out at night in search of food.

As you might expect, officials are investigating all aspects of this case. Apparently, the police and teachers were aware of the situation but unable to act. Two caseworkers involved with the three children have been fired. The article disclosed that Nicole Finn is *"facing a charge of first-degree murder for Natalie's death and several other felonies for her treatment of two of Natalie's siblings"* while Joe *"is facing several charges of kidnapping, neglect or abandonment and child endangerment."*

This is a horrible story with an even sadder ending for a young teenager who never got to go to her senior prom or to graduate with her friends. It's possible that had other relatives been found, this tragedy could have been avoided. Natalie might still be alive if she, her sister and brother had been placed with an aunt or grandparent. Yet no news story has explained much about Natalie's birth parents so we can only speculate on whether relative placement was possible.

When children enter foster care, society has a contract through our government agencies to protect and help these innocent kids. As a society we failed Natalie. Finding a foster child's relatives and placing the child with them is not a silver bullet, but in most cases, being with family is preferable to being sent to live with strangers. On the other hand, adoption is an important and sometimes the only alternative for a foster child other than their spending years languishing in a government institution. There are tens of thousands of parents who do love and care for their adoptive child. Sadly, Natalie was not given to such parents. We must do more because foster children deserve so much better.

I've posted about foster child abuse on Facebook. I've often wondered how the public views certain words. For instance, if you read the word "abuse," what image comes to mind? Maybe you think of a teenage being slapped. Perhaps you picture a child being shoved. Your idea of abuse is based in part on your upbringing, so if you grew up in a family where people didn't yell, then being screamed at might be your idea of abuse. You may not have been in a family where an older brother would constantly punch you or an older sister would make your life miserable. Those actions might be your idea of abuse.

Yet the abuse that thousands of foster youths suffer is much more extreme. To bring the word "abuse" to life, we posted the following on social media:

> *"While you read this, a foster child as young as four years old may be getting hit, slapped, kicked, thrown into a wall, molested or even raped."*

Now, your idea of abuse may have immediately shifted after you read that post. There's less room to wonder what the word "abuse" means because it's spelled out. This post received both praise and criticism from former foster kids. One wrote, *"You need to edit this, as a former foster youth I am offended by your description. I think that is salacious."*

Yet another former foster kid had this to say:

> *"There's nothing wrong with the original post. I'm also a survivor of the system – I spent my entire childhood in foster care: 10 placements in 20 years – and I'm personally beyond done with this trend toward whitewashing the lived experiences of foster kids in the name of good PR. I appreciate Forever Homes for Foster Kids' openness about the darker side of the system that so many other foster care pages won't touch because it's not pleasant or inspiring. Social media discourse on foster care focuses way too much on making non-fosters feel comfortable and self-satisfied. Maybe we need to start making the public feel more uncomfortable*

with the way things are for so many foster kids, so that they will be moved to change things instead of patting themselves on the back while kids are literally dying in care."

That's a reality check! While it may be shocking to hear about abuse in plain language, foster children need the public to wake up.

There was a firestorm in Hollywood revolving around accusations of sexual harassment, molestation and even rape against workers, actresses and even actors. Both men and women stepped up to tell stories about their abuse. You may have heard about the many allegations of sexual abuse and rape brought against Harvey Weinstein, co-founder of Miramax Films and an award-winning producer. While his behavior had been an open secret in Hollywood for years, it took an exposé by The New York Times to break the story wide open.

Several of Weinstein's accusers were some of Hollywood's top stars: Angelina Jolie, Ashley Judd, Kate Beckinsale and Gwyneth Paltrow. Some actresses, such as Rose McGowan, had previously agreed to settlements related to their abuse by Weinstein. Many celebrities and leaders spoke out about the abuse.

The floodgates appeared to be open with other stars having been named for alleged abuses, and some complaints being leveled at politicians. But even with all this information of abuse suddenly visible in the media, it seemed it was still not time for someone to speak out about the abuses of foster children. The actresses who stepped up to talk about their abuse were some of the most financially and professionally successful adults in the world. Compare their position to the thousands of foster kids who do not have money, position, or power.

These kids have learned from experience that they often cannot turn to adults such as the police, a doctor or teacher because their stories most likely won't be believed.

While my original Facebook post focused on the abuse happening to some foster children, many adults and foster parents joined the conversation. Most expressed attitudes similar to this one, something that you would probably expect from a caring foster parent:

> "I have been a foster parent for almost seven years, and I would never harm a child in any way. I do not understand how anybody could do that to a child/ren."

A couple of other foster parents commented:

> "What about all the foster children who are being loved, nurtured, clothed, & provided a stable home! Great selfless foster parents sacrifice their lives to care for children."

> "Please shine a little good light on foster care instead of negative, we need good parents and good homes to stop homes like you are always talking about."

Yes, most foster parents are doing a good job, but many more need to know about the statistics concerning foster care abuse.

Part of our social media focus is to highlight these sad realities to inform the public, government officials and foster parents as to facts that otherwise may never be seen or heard. The hard truth is that change does not happen when everything seems sunny and rosy. It's only when the harsh realities are revealed that people take notice, and that notice can lead to change.

Another post on Facebook read:

> *"Although those of us providing loving foster homes would not disagree that the system has many flaws, I can't help but feel that many of your posts are bashing foster parents. If you truly are about educating on the need for better foster homes, it seems you might pick your stories and comments more carefully."*

This individual and a few others voiced an opinion about "selective" topics, meaning censuring dialogue about those topics and stories not deemed to be politically correct. That opinion above is not unique, but this next comment really caught our attention:

> *"I am so done with this page and all of its inaccurate representations of the foster system."*

The person who posted this response and others like him ARE part of the problem. Too many foster parents, when they hear about those who are doing harm to foster children, take stories like the one I posted as an affront to their own good works. Worse are those adults, some of whom are not even directly involved with foster care, who go even further and publicly deny that these abuses exist. They don't simply want the truth hidden. They want to paint the truth as false or fake news. Through their public denial, these people are victimizing foster children all over again because they are actively working to silence these children's voices of pain by asserting that these abuses do not occur rather than addressing the alarming reality.

Martin Luther King wrote, *"There comes a time when silence is betrayal."* Whether a foster parent or not, anyone who is either quiet or, worse, publicly denies the suffering and pain of foster children as "inaccuracies" is someone who has, as Desmond Tutu wrote, *"chosen the side of the oppressor."*

Foster children may find no refuge even in schools - where they are forced to confront bullying by others. A recent survey asked former foster children if they had been harassed in school. Some of the responses were:

> *"I was. A lot of the boys physically hurt me, and girls would be really mean."*

> *"Yes, I was bullied by one girl in high school who was my friend. When I told her I was in foster care, everything changed. She would say things like 'at least my parents love me' and 'at least I have a family.' I had heaps of kids in primary school do the same. Their favorite line was 'at least my parents love me.'"*

> *"When girls in middle school found out, they were brutal. Needless to say, it made life a lot harder."*

> *"I was treated differently by teachers and bullied by the popular girls in town. I would skip school just to not have to put up with it every day."*

> *"I remember that birthday invitations were handed out to every girl in class but me. 'Her foster mother*

won't let her go to anyone's house anyway,' the
girl announced to the class."

These experiences are all to common and cruel.

Classmates are a huge challenge for many foster kids because fellow students can be verbally and physically abusive. Other comments described the parents of fellow students making derogatory remarks or going out of their way to remind the foster child that they were different or delinquent.

Some foster children wrote about having to fight back and getting into trouble for defending themselves while a few wrote how they started to become a bully themselves. Others talked about having run away and living on the street or overdosing on pills and ending up in an intensive care unit, all to get away from the physical and emotional pain they experienced at school.

Teachers can be the one who lets classmates know that a child is in foster care. They may learn about a foster child because when that child is enrolled, the school will receive required legal documents for identification. A birth certificate can easily signal that a child is not related to the parents. One school administrator said that common sense should dictate that talking about a student's personal life is improper unless there is a medical emergency.

However, for whatever reason sometimes a teacher will tell a foster kid's classmates about them. Then the bullying begins. I recently sat down with a high school teacher, who had 17 years of experience. I told her how many foster teens are afraid of being found out at school. She replied, *"Most kids are too self-absorbed to care if a fellow student is a foster teen."*

As the quotes from former foster children show, her observations couldn't be further from the truth. I relayed her comments to several former foster kids who shared that hers was not an uncommon attitude. Therein lies a serious part of the problem for foster children. When educated, experienced teachers are so out of touch with the lives of their students, these kids will eventually lose trust in another important authority figure.

We have all heard at least one story of an athlete or successful businessperson who credited their success with having had a coach or teacher during their childhood who cared enough to work with and support them. But foster children are often deprived of this opportunity by the ignorance of their teachers. Some teachers have turned against a foster child by embarrassing them to their classmates and putting the kid potentially in harm's way. Many foster kids are already traumatized by how they were removed from their home. Teachers, administrators and foster parents may be harming a child either directly or through indifference.

Debra, a former foster youth who now works for her school district, shared that when teachers didn't want to deal with a foster care kid, the principal would be summoned and would take the student to their office even if the child had done nothing disruptive in class.

Somehow the public in general expects these kids to look past all that hurt and abuse and believe in adults who have already shown they are clearly not to be trusted. Fortunately, some foster children do find refuge with a teacher. Lisa, a former foster kid, wrote, *"I was bullied several times. That's why I kept close to the teachers."*

Even if a foster child does find a protective and sympathetic teacher, the child will have to spend some time alone with other students. Former foster kids have reported being attacked in restrooms and on the playground.

School administrators sometimes instigate abuse and harassment. Allan, a former foster youth, shared this story.

> *"My senior year, I was transferred to a foster home in Georgia. My foster mother took my foster brother and me to the school about a week before school started to meet with the principal. He sat us down and gave us a lecture on how he knew we were foster kids and would be watching us. If we caused problems, he would have our asses. We were both in foster care because of abusive parents."*

Foster care was never meant to take the place of a loving family. Getting children out of the system quickly is critically important. Thorough family finding often gives a child a permanent, forever family. While placement with a relative doesn't always guarantee a happy ending, it must be the urgent intent of foster care agencies to work to place a foster child with their family whenever possible.

Chapter Twelve

Ongoing Crisis in Texas of Foster Child Harm and Death

Today Texas has what can aptly be called one of the worst foster care systems in the United States. I first became aware of some of the state's foster care issues in 2014 when my nonprofit began receiving multiple inquiries from CPS' offices across Texas. One of the most surprising phone calls that we received was from a CPS official in Edinberg, Texas. She explained that Texas CPS had identified a number of cases involving Latino children with family in Mexico and possibly other countries in Latin America. These cases had been languishing for many years but were now being given a high priority.

This Edinberg official went on to explain that Texas CPS was creating three offices that would specialize in performing family finding for these cases. The best outcome would be that a relative would be located and notified and would then come forward and take the child giving them a forever home. This official was calling

Forever Homes because she was looking for assistance on how to locate relatives in Latin America. Even though Texas foster care agencies were at the time handling many cases involving Latino children who had relatives in Mexico, the need still existed for an elite class of caseworkers with specialized family finding experience. If the head of such a foster care agency was calling for assistance so they could successfully complete their mission, one can only imagine how challenging it must have been for foster care agencies in Texas and other border states that did not have access to professionals with such specialized skills.

In 2015, I finally had the opportunity to talk with the head of Texas CPS. It was not a fruitful conversation because the official kept saying, *"We have it handled."* I tried to explain diplomatically that they did not have anything handled. We were taking on cases from all across Texas. We were handling multiple cases sometimes from different departments in the same building. I told the official about the phone call we had received from the Edinberg office, and she still continued to tell me that they had everything handled.

When I was doing international marketing, one of the easiest tipoffs that the person I was dealing with had no clue as to how to conduct business in Latin America was when they would tell me, *"We have it handled."* That short sentence is so full of arrogance, and maybe stupidity, because no one has it handled when it comes to Latin America. I've been working with Latin America for nearly 30 years, have given presentations about marketing, communication and inclusivity at universities in both the United States and Mexico, and I am still learning something new every week about the culture, countries, politics or process in Latin America.

Later that year U.S. District Judge Janis Jack initiated court oversight over the Texas foster care system due to years of mismanagement that have and continue to put hundreds of the state's foster children at risk. Her involvement was prompted in part by a 2011 lawsuit brought against the Texas Department of Family and Protective Services on behalf of several foster children.

Each year more than a hundred foster children die while in Texas foster care or after they are released back to their parent or guardian. It is very challenging to root out abuses and neglect in foster care due to the secrecy that surrounds the system. On the one hand, the state is obligated to protect the identity of children who have been abused so that their abusers are not able to find them. This cloak of protection also prevents good oversight that could catch instances of neglect, prejudice and abuse by caseworkers and management.

In the June 2016 Houston Chronicle article, "Judge beefs up plan to fix foster care," Andrea Zelinski reported on the judge's latest effort to address the governmental disaster known as Texas foster care. Judge Jack had just approved a research plan to find solutions to the state's foster children crisis. Judge Jack tapped child experts to compile a list of actions that, once completed, would ensure that Texas foster children would receive the care and protections that they are due. Nine experts weighed in on the then-existing system and submitted their findings and recommendations.

The article continued that Judge Jack noted in a *"scathing 255-page order that children in Texas foster care 'almost uniformly leave state custody more damaged than when they entered.' She found that 'rape, abuse, psychotropic medication, and instability are the norm,' that child-on-child abuse in licensed foster care placements is common but not tracked, and that children who rape other children continue to do it as they relocate to new homes."*

Judge Jack found that: *"caseloads range from unsustainable to unbearable with workers often juggling some 30 cases at a time, burning out nearly one in five workers every year. Paul Yetter, a Houston lawyer leading the challenge against the foster care system on behalf of children in long term care agreed saying, Caseworkers are literally buried in work and just too busy to keep children safe. Without manageable caseloads, innocent children are at risk. Everyone knows this. State officials have said the ideal caseload is between 18-22."*

The judge has often called the Texas foster care system "broken." With all due respect to the judge, calling this system "broken" severely understates the outrageous ongoing damage and criminal activity that has continued against the state's children. In this context, the word "broken" really is a sugar-coated way of saying *"environment where rapists and pedophiles are allowed to attack foster children with little to no fear of prosecution."*

In a 2019 article "Federal Judge in Texas Fines CPS $50K a Day for 'Shameful' Foster Care: CPS has 'Lied to Me at Almost Every Level'," reporter Brian Shilhavy wrote that Texas foster children are under Permanent Managing Conservatorship (PMC). Judge Jack stated:

"Texas's foster care system is broken, and it has been that way for decades. It is broken for all stakeholders, including DFPS [Department of Family and Protective Services] employees who are tasked with impossible workloads. Most importantly, though, it is broken for Texas's PMC children, who almost uniformly leave State custody more damaged than when they entered."

One of the shocking aspects of the state system is that some children brought into foster care are placed in group homes where there is no 24-hour supervision. Imagine having your child at a daycare where the adults left the children alone for an hour or two. Anyone who has ever been around a 2-year-old knows it takes only seconds for a child to get into a possibly life-threatening situation. Yet, traumatized children who had been taken from their homes were being placed in a strange house with other kids and, at some point, being left alone.

A 2018 article by Keri Blakinger gave a shocking example of the deplorable practices that tear Texas families apart by highlighting a case where a Houston CPS worker and his supervisor were found guilty of taking two children from their parents – a 2-year-old daughter and 5-month-old son – through lies and deceit. *"In a scathing ruling from the bench, Juvenile Court Judge Mike Schneider dinged the agency for being 'dishonest' and possibly 'malicious.'"* The damages awarded to the parents were $127,000, the largest such award ever in Texas. The amount could have been greater except that the judge didn't want to overload Texas taxpayers, who will essentially be footing the bill.

Other serious deficiencies within Texas CPS include the use of visitation workers to supplement work performed by trained CPS staff. According to a November 2018 article by Robert T. Garrett of The Dallas Morning News, federal law and state policy require caseworkers to see an individual foster child each month. However, Texas has contracts with about 100 non-full-fledged CPS caseworkers.

These workers were hired to check on remotely placed foster kids. Judge Jack had written that although someone was visiting the children, these visits are essentially a token effort to *"confirm that the child 'is still there.'"* She said, *"Children don't feel comfortable sharing their problems with the rotating roster of 'I See You' workers, who often fail to meet with them in private as required. 'I See You' workers are clearly not equipped to be caseworkers. They were never part of the court process or planning for the outcome of the child."*

The November article revealed that more than 12,000 children are in long-term state foster care. Unfortunately, the more time a child spends in foster care, the greater their risk of abuse. When foster kids reach age 13, their chances of leaving the system by adoption drops to nearly 1%, meaning that thousands of Texas foster children will be calling state institutions and group facilities their home for many years.

There have been some improvements since 2011 when Judge Jack first became involved with Texas foster care, but the state still remains under court oversight for failing to institute most of the required changes. In a January 2022 Spectrum News 1 article, attorney Paul Yetter said:

"It's about leadership, it's about better use of the funds. The leadership between the two main agencies have been at odds, [so] the funds they are getting are being wasted. And some of the funds they could be getting from the federal government are sitting idle, because the state is not doing what it needs to do to get those funds. There was a number of unsafe facilities that they [Texas] closed, which was a good thing. Yet they didn't replace them with safe facilities." The article cited an example where *"a facility in Michigan housing Texas kids was without a door and had no heat for over 24 hours, despite the temperature being below freezing."*

It was also revealed that Judge *"Jack also ripped into CPS for other failings, like not being able to track all the kids in their care."*

You've read about the many benefits of family finding. Texas had 47,913 children in foster care in 2020. According to The Imprint that tracks foster care payments in Texas, the maximum monthly cost paid for a child cared for by a relative, referred to as "kinship care," is "$406 per month for up to one year, plus a $500 annual stipend for a maximum three years, or until the child's 18th birthday. Monthly foster care payments in Texas range from $812 to $2,773 per child" for a foster parent. If we took just 1,000 of those children (2%), located their relatives, removed the kids from a group home care, which could cost roughly $2.7 million annually, and instead put them into kinship care at a cost of about $411,000, the State of Texas and its taxpayers could have saved $2.2 million.

The positive impact of placing foster children with relatives is so important that the Annie E. Casey Foundation, one of the country's largest and most prestigious foster children nonprofits, created a three-minute video, "Every Kid Needs a Family: A Message to Caseworkers." Former foster children share and plead with caseworkers to *"persist in connecting teens with family — because every teen needs a family."*

The Texas governor and attorney general are both Republicans, and most Republican government officials might salivate at the thought of less government while saving more than $2.2 million. That's a win-win that any politician can embrace. Now what if the governor made Texas the role model for foster care reform instead of fighting against changes? It's doable because, sadly, few states have so much to work with as does Texas. If the state did make even mediocre improvements, those would look amazing compared to the broken system that exists right now.

No matter which side of the aisle your representative sits on, successfully caring for foster children is good for everyone. Democrats can love the outcome of saving children from harm and placing them with relatives where the kids can now have stability and love. Republicans can embrace the results because it means less government bloat and better use of public funds while still giving foster children a chance at a brighter future with the love and support of family.

Texas lawmakers must step up and make the necessary changes for the wellbeing of all the children in the state. Change can happen quickly with the stroke of a governor's pen. Foster children deserve so much better, and there is no reason they can't have a better, safer future starting this week.

Chapter Thirteen

Foster Children Reunification Success Stories

How do you measure success when you're finding the families of foster children? It's not as simple as reunification. Though that's the goal, each child's story and circumstances are different. Our successful outcomes are shown through the lives we've changed and the positive impacts on the children we've helped. Below you'll find a few of the letters we've received from grateful foster care agencies who have shared their experiences with us. And, more importantly, they demonstrate how successful family finding has changed the lives of real children in a multitude of tangible ways.

*   *   *

Dear Richard,

On behalf of Ventura County Children and Family Services, I would like to thank you for the work your organization did in searching for the relatives of a pair of siblings in Mexico. As you know this was a very complex case, and we had little information to go on. Your agency was exceptionally thorough and persistent in working to identify and locate family for these two children.

These children have been in foster care for 10 years without knowing the whereabouts of either of their parents. Because of this abandonment they have both experienced significant trauma that has hampered their ability to function and thrive. Now suddenly everything has changed.

As a result of these search efforts, both parents have been found along with a rich extended family of grandparents, aunts, uncles and cousins. The children have been in contact with many of them and are eagerly anticipating a trip to Mexico to meet them. Their prospects for the future now look very different, and they feel a sense of identity and belonging they never had before.

This is not the first time I have used your services. Each time I have called upon Forever Homes for Foster Kids, I have been delighted with the service I have received. As a family finding expert, I don't know of any other service that comes close to doing what Forever Homes for Foster Kids does. You are truly saving lives.

I look forward to continuing to work with you in the future and would not hesitate in referring your services to others. Once again, thank you.

Best,

Jill Borgeson, MSW
Family Finding and Engagement
Ventura County Children and Family Services
Oxnard, California 93033

Can you imagine what it must be like to feel so lost and abandoned for most of your childhood? No warm hugs when you are sad. No loving words from close family members to remind you that you belong and are wanted. Feeling separated from a shared family and cultural history, all while wondering where you belong. And can you imagine how painful it would be to not know where your parents are or why you aren't able to be with them?

Each year, thousands of kids in the U.S. are abandoned by a parent or guardian and are too young to help caseworkers to locate their relatives. The siblings in the story above could easily have stayed in foster care and been separated into different foster homes or even adopted by different families. When this happens, some kids never see their brothers or sisters again.

Against all odds, this was an amazing outcome for these two foster kids. Now their future is so much brighter... Or as Jill wrote, "they feel a sense of identity and belonging they never had before." Belonging isn't just about being in a home. It's about feeling the love of family and feeling safe. For these two kids and their mother, family finding made this reunion after 10 years apart possible. We improved the lives of these beautiful children with a sense of social connection that has both social benefit and financial benefit for these kids as well as the community.

*   *   *

Dear Mr. Villasana:

I am writing to express my profound gratitude for the services that your organization provided on behalf of Deborah M, an 18-year-old Los Angeles County foster child. One of Deborah's greatest wishes was to establish a connection with her birth father who was reported to be living in Mexico. The judge in Deborah's case ordered the department to conduct family finding services, and I assigned the case to myself because all of my team members had a full caseload.

DCFS has a well-established family finding operation that has developed various search methods for locating parents and relatives. Nonetheless, after conducting an extensive search for Deborah's father, I could not locate him. I felt terrible because I had promised Deborah that I would leave no stone unturned in my search for her dad. Then, one day as I sat down at my desk, I found a magazine article that someone had left on my desk about an organization that has had much success in finding relatives of foster children living in Mexico.

My initial contact with Forever Homes for Foster Kids was to obtain advice on how I might conduct a better search for Deborah's father, which you gladly provided. I then obtained approval to utilize your organization's services in searching for Deborah's father and was able to learn just how much expertise you have in conducting such searches. It was very exciting for both Deborah and me to read the reports detailing the results of your family finding efforts and although Deborah's father was not found (or he decided not to respond to the letters that I sent to him), it was most rewarding to have Deborah tell me how much she appreciated the work that was done by your organization and by my department on her behalf.

As I continue my work as a family finding supervisor, I can assure you that your organization will always be my go-to resource when all else fails in my search for the parents and relatives of the foster children and youth whom we serve.

Best regards,

Robert La Farge, MSW
Supervising Children's Social Worker
Department of Children and Family Services
County of Los Angeles
Los Angeles, California 90020

Can you picture growing up in a system that controls every aspect of your life? You're assigned to case workers and homes. If you're lucky, you get placed somewhere you feel safe and loved. But, for no reason at all, you can be torn away. What went wrong? Were you bad? Your caseworker is someone new; maybe they don't have time to even talk with you. It doesn't take long before you feel like just another case number, a file buried in a mountain of other forgotten children.

Several former foster kids have shared that they aged out having felt that no one heard them or cared enough to do a thorough family finding. These kids feel abandoned and lied to by a system that promises to care for them and do its best for each child. Instead, family finding often gives a foster kid a sense of peace knowing that people were doing everything possible to make reunification a reality. That effort tells a child they are valued. They have worth, and few things are so appreciated and important to a child than knowing they were a top priority.

As mentioned in this letter, Deborah's father was most likely found and notified, but he never responded back. Even though our work did not result in Deborah being reunited with her father, she knew that someone took her case seriously and did everything possible to find him. She felt seen. Her needs were recognized. And she knew every possible step was taken to try to reunite them. Going into adulthood, she is able to carry with her the confidence that she was more than just a case number on a file. She had value.

*   *   *

Dear Mr. Villasana,

On behalf of the American Civil Liberties Union, we thank you and your charity for your efforts in Honduras to locate a parent who was separated from their child. Our organization has led the fight to reunite the thousands of parents who had their children taken away at the Mexico-U.S. border in recent years. The ACLU has dedicated enormous resources to reconnect these parents with their children.

Despite more than two thousand successful reunifications, some mothers and fathers still remain apart from their children, worrying about their health and safety, and desperate to hold their child again. One of the greatest obstacles to successfully locating a parent in Honduras is the limited information we have on file from the U.S. government about the parent.

Earlier this year, we retained Forever Homes for Foster Kids because of your organization's expertise in finding relatives in countries throughout Latin America, including Honduras. Forever Homes for Foster Kids has proven effective in engaging with officials who provide their time and resources to locate a parent.

In this particular case, ongoing efforts had failed to locate the mother, so the ACLU called upon your services. Within just weeks of receiving the case information, your organization identified the mother and provided us with her contact information.

Without your services, we would not have the critical information to be able to communicate with this mother. Our ultimate goal is that she has the choice to reunite with her child and live in the U.S.

The ACLU greatly appreciates your dedication and diligence to a successful conclusion for this case as well as for the many other cases that Forever Homes for Foster Kids has resolved in Honduras for our organization.

Sincerely,

Daniel Galindo
Staff Attorney, Immigrants' Rights Project
New York, New York 10004

Let's say you're a young child traveling with your mother away from the only home you've ever known. You get to the border and are surrounded by intimidating officials. Then you're ripped from your mother's arms and separated from her. She's the only person you know, the only friendly or familiar face. You're reaching for your mom and crying, but no one listens.

This didn't happen for just 30 minutes or a few hours. Months went by without their mother while a little boy or girl sat on a mat or benches, only allowed outside for 30 minutes each day. No hug. No smile. No "I love you." Not a single loved one who knows just the right bedtime story to make sure the nightmares stay away.

These innocent children just want to be held again by their father or mother. They want to feel safe and loved. A child may not understand why they are separated from their parent; they only know that they miss them and every day just want to be back with their family. Locating a child's parent is the only way to make this reunion possible.

It has been an honor to apply our expertise to locating many parents who were separated from their children at the Mexico-U.S. border in 2017 and 2018. It takes time, expertise, and money to find that missing mom or dad. Donations make it possible for a child to see their parent soon.

*   *   *

Dear Mr. Villasana,

On behalf of the Chester County Children, Youth and Families, I sincerely thank you for your specialized family finding expertise. We had three young sisters in our care in Pennsylvania, far away from their family in Mexico, with no direct contact information. We were at a loss to know how to begin a search for their relatives.

Your company successfully navigated through extraordinary obstacles and found the contact information that had long eluded us. The relatives of the three sisters were thought to live in small, remote villages with no telephone service, no Internet, and no cellphone reception. You were able to arrange for someone to drive into each village in search of these relatives. You located a grandfather, and then an aunt who lived in a large Mexican city many states over. We consider your company's ability to track down members of this family under these circumstances as nothing short of miraculous.

We never imagined that the news would get better, but it did. We have since learned that there are family members living in the northeast USA. We knew of them but had never been able to locate them. There is strong evidence that we will be more than able to reach the daughters' birth father. At last, we now have several options for the girls. These children may very well end up in a permanent home with one of their relatives.

We simply wouldn't have these family connections in both Mexico and the U.S. without your expertise. Your organization has been a blessing in disguise for these young foster children and our agency. We know that we can count on your organization for any additional assistance.

Again, accept our most sincere appreciation for the superb work your organization provided to our foster children.

With warmest regards,

Carmen Rivera
Chester County Department of Children, Youth and Families
West Chester, Pennsylvania 19380

Imagine you're a child in a strange country without your parents. Your only sense of familiarity and stability is through your connection to your two sisters, both of whom feel just as lost as you do. Clinging to the only family you have left, you may all be sent from home to home. But you never know if, in the next move, they will be taken away from you too.

Every family finding case is unique. Not only were these three sisters at risk of being separated, but without that sense of belonging with family, their future was bleak. Fifty percent of girls who are forced out of foster care at 18 become pregnant by age 19. Being raised in foster care increases the likelihood of early pregnancy, as does the lack of close family connections. Misdirected sexual activity can also be a method of securing shelter and creating a sense of family when there are no other supports to fall back on.

Because these girls are often homeless, they can't get proper medical care. Some states are now forcing children to go through full-term pregnancies. These kids, who were the responsibility of the state, now fight to get food, supplements, and a stress-free, healthy environment to even have a safe pregnancy. A former foster teen can easily die from preeclampsia, extreme high blood pressure, during pregnancy. Imagine the terror of going through a pregnancy alone with no mother or aunt to help. How frightening would it be to have no one to hold your hand, reassure you or support you through that life-changing process when you are barely more than a child yourself?

These girls could be your sister, daughter, or niece. They're children fighting to survive in a system that was never designed to help them... Never given the tools or support necessary to equip them to navigate or thrive in adult life outside of foster care, these kids are desperately trying to find ways to survive however they can.

Because of our family finding effort, these three girls don't have to live with the possibility of being separated, aging out, being on welfare or dying from pregnancy. Instead, these three sisters are in a loving home with a family member. They'll be less likely to engage in criminal activities, be disengaged from school, or become pregnant because they now have that sense of security and belonging. Our work makes these kids feel safer and loved because they now have a true family. And those bonds give them the support and ability to make better choices.

*   *   *

Dear Mr. Richard Villasana,

I am writing to express my profound gratitude for the services that your organization provided on behalf of Yolanda A, a 14-year-old York County, Pennsylvania, foster child. One of her greatest wishes was to reconnect with her birth parents who were reported to be living in Honduras. The judge and county workers ordered family finding services, and I was assigned to the case because I was bilingual, and Yolanda speaks only Spanish. Yet finding her birth parents in her hometown with her young mind of remembering names of towns close to home was very upsetting as we had little hope and not knowing where to start.

Yolanda had little information to give about the location and any specific names of her hometown and spellings. Her family as she remembers has little to nothing when it comes to access to technology. Our goal of finding/locating them or a contact to reach them was mostly unreachable until my supervisor Elisa had told me about your organization and how you were able to help Yolanda locate information and some connections to her relatives. When we received your email with her father's contact, she was over-the-top thrilled to finally have a contact for her birth father. The county worker and Yolanda's team of workers were also very glad to have a phone number to reach her birth father and mother who reside together, to be able to communicate with them about Yolanda's case and moving toward permanency with a foster family in the states.

It was most rewarding to have Yolanda tell me how much she appreciated the work you have done and your organization and by my department on her behalf, we would like to say THANK YOU!

Sincerely,

Nelly Velez
PA Child Permanency Division
Harrisburg, Pennsylvania 17101

What would it be like to be alone in a strange country and unable to speak the primary language? How much more isolated would you feel being unable to communicate easily with the very people assigned to your case? Would you know if they truly understood you? Could you trust that they were advocating for your best interests? Now imagine that experience as a child trying to find a way home, who only remembers the vaguest of details.

PA Child is an outstanding nonprofit located in the state of Pennsylvania. Yolanda was fortunate that her case was passed to PA Child that has Spanish-speaking caseworkers such as Nelly Velez. Yolanda was *"over-the-top thrilled to finally have a contact for her birth father."*

Time and time again, we hear this same theme. Every child feels this way when they know they are leaving foster care to finally see their mom or dad and be with them. When a foster child is back in touch with actual family members, that child is more likely to feel that sense of belonging. With connections and roots to ground them, they are better able to live a happy, healthy, thriving life.

In foster care, Yolanda's grim future was probably homelessness. She may have turned to prostitution to make ends meet or heavy drug use to numb the pain. Ultimately, either path could end in prison. Now she has a much better chance to finish high school, go to college, have a great career, and contribute to both her family and the community.

The goal of family reunification is to give this better future to each child we help.

*   *   *

Dear Mr. Villasana,

We reached out to Forever Home for Foster Kids in hopes of finding family for a youth that had very little information on her roots. Because the youth resides in the States with very few familial contacts, this felt like our last hope. I did not have much information on family names and even had the misspelling of the ones I requested a search for.

Through diligence, Forever Homes for Foster Kids searched families with similar names and was able to find two family members. The findings have been helpful in answering the youth's questions and finding more pieces of her puzzle. The family member wants communication with the youth, and we are happy to say that grim situation just got brighter!

It is our human right and need to know who our family is and what happened to us. The emptiness that having unanswered questions creates is bitter turmoil and grief. There are many challenges and sadness in the world but not knowing who your family is and essentially who you are shouldn't be one that children are facing.

Melissa Ruano
YMCA Permanent Connections
San Diego, California 92116

What fills the gap when you don't have a sense of identity or community to anchor you? And when you don't know your own story or how you came to be where you are, how do you fill in those gaps? How can you move forward? These are hard questions for most adults to answer after a lifetime of experiences. It's heartbreaking that so many children must wrestle with them before they can process the grief of a loss they can barely understand themselves.

A child who doesn't know who they are, or have that sense of belonging, often turns bitter. They feel unloved and unwanted, creating a foundation for violence against themselves and others. For foster children, this deeply intense personal pain is heightened by a system that shuffles them around from home to home without care. It's easy for them to believe the idea that they are unworthy. It becomes part of their truth and identity, influencing every aspect of their lives and every choice they make.

They're hurting. Sometimes the bitterness is turned inwards. Other times it's used as a weapon to keep others at bay. But as they walk through life and interact with others, their pain doesn't stay their own. Society suffers as a whole. All of this because they are denied human connections to their family, their story, and their sense of belonging.

Finding a family member is the key to completely changing a child's outcome. No longer alone, a child will have family support. Sadly, while not every child's relatives will take them in, the family may still provide financial support. At the very least, a child will have emotional family support. For many foster children, that will be enough to get them through the toughest times.

Family finding is not just about giving a foster child a roof or a hot meal. It's about providing that child that sense of belonging and social connection. We want every child to live happy, healthy, educated, and abuse-free lives. Our family finding work makes this possible and donations make this happen. Our work is not paid for by foster care agencies. People just like you give to be part of the solution so a child will have a better future and know they are a welcome part of their community.

*   *   *

Dear Mr. Villasana,

I want to thank you and your organization for your assistance with locating family members for children in care whom I was providing services.

Here at Family Finding at Turning Points for Children, we do not have the access to be able to search for family members outside of the U.S. In this case, your services were needed as the family is from Brazil.

The father in this case was taking care of 16, 15, and 7-year-old sons and a 6-year-old daughter on his own while working full time in construction to provide for his family. The Community Umbrella Agency offering services to him did not know of any family members who could help, and he was struggling. Utilizing the results and information from your inquiries, we were able to locate a paternal aunt and her family, who immediately offered to help the father in any way. We were also able to locate the paternal grandmother of the children who stated she was able and willing to visit with the children weekly after work and babysit.

Without the information your agency obtained, we would not have been able to locate these supports for the family. Father and the children are currently connected with these family supports, and they are actively helping to take care of the children.

Once again, I would like to thank you for your diligence with this case. We at Family Finding will continue to reach out to Forever Homes for Foster Kids and recommend other organizations to do so as well.

Sincerely,

Danielle White
Family Finding Case Manager
Turning Points for Children
Philadelphia, Pennsylvania 19146

You might wonder what could happen if families were never separated. How would the outcomes be different? Sometimes we receive a case, such as this one, where a caseworker is trying to keep a family together. This single parent was struggling to give his children a good home. Relatives were located who were eager and willing to help the family. This case is an excellent example of how preventative intervention can keep a family together and make it stronger.

Imagine this father's fear that he could lose his kids, or because he was stretched so thin, that one of his kids could get sick or hurt and he wouldn't be there for them. Picture the sleepless nights worrying about the worst-case scenarios, knowing he had no backup plan or help. Belonging is critically important, but so is having a parent who is there for the kids. This dad wanted to be with his kids and just needed some support. Finding his relatives gave him that assistance, mitigating a lot of emotional and financial stress from this desperate single parent.

The kids now get to spend time with their grandmother, who will hopefully spoil them. She'll tell them how proud she is of them and how special they are, which is what every child wants to hear. Because their father has a supportive family to help, his stress is reduced and he likely has more energy to devote to his kids. This will help raise their self-esteem and sense of worth. These kids having more time with their dad and other relatives is an outcome worth being a part of. That's the work we do for a child by finding family members.

*   *   *

Dear Mr. Villasana,

I want to thank your organization for its work in helping locate family members of a child under our agency's care. Our options on this case were very limited, and therefore we reached out to Forever Homes for Foster Kids.

It is my understanding that your organization spent several months working to locate relatives in Mexico due in part to the limited information we could provide. Surprisingly, I started receiving phone calls last Friday from the child's family members including the mother. We are now very hopeful that the child can be reunited and placed with either a parent or a close relative.

It's clear that from your work of having a relative located and interviewed in Mexico that other family members were contacted and advised that they had a relative in foster care. Our agency would definitely use your services on future cases and would recommend Forever Homes for Foster

Kids to other agencies in need of locating relatives in Mexico and Central America.

Sincerely,

Jaime R. Hernandez
Child Protective Services Specialist II
Texas Department of Family and Protective Services
Arlington, Texas 76011

What would it mean to you if one day you were all alone in the world, and the next you learned you were part of a loving family that wanted you? This foster child was all alone. As far as they knew, they had no family. When I called and spoke to Jaime, he was very excited because he had received so many calls on Friday from family members. What would it feel like to be able to give the child that wonderful news and see their eyes light up when they realized they weren't alone?

When a child is back with family, they feel loved, safe, and connected. That child now has a sense of belonging. They're more engaged in school. And they're less likely to be abused or bullied. With a support system and a loving family, they can safely process the trauma from being in the foster system and deal with it in healthy ways.

Want a better society? It starts with having children who feel loved and protected. Every penny that goes into finding a child's relatives is worthwhile. This child went from feeling alone to having several relatives calling about them. All that was needed was for these relatives to be found and notified.

*   *   *

Dear Mr. Villasana,

On behalf of Casa Pacifica, I sincerely thank you for your specialized family finding service. You located the aunt and other relatives of a child in our care in an obscure part of Mexico. Your organization successfully navigated through extraordinary obstacles and found direct contact information that had long eluded us. Happily, this allowed us to reach the child's family and re-establish a connection and a long-term bond with his only known relatives.

As you know, our nonprofit is contracted with Ventura County to perform, among many responsibilities, family finding for the children in foster care. The desired outcome is that by finding family members, a child can be placed in a permanent home with loving relatives. Family finding requires us to locate as many relatives as possible. In this way we can eventually identify those family members who will give the child the family connection he/she needs.

The particular case that your organization handled involved a child whose relatives live in a town of less than 200 people with no telephone service, no Internet, and no cell phone reception. Rosie Lopez, Case Manager, was shocked that your charity had any success at all because of the town's remote location and was "so happy" with the results. We consider your organization's ability to track down members of this family under these circumstances as nothing short of miraculous. We have already started the process to reconnect this child with an aunt on the mother's side of the family.

You have proven your services to us in several cases, none of which we had been able to make progress based on our own resources. We are confident that we can count on your continued services in locating family members for other foster children who have relatives still living in Mexico.

Again, accept our most sincere appreciation for the work your organization provides to our foster children.

With warmest regards,

Jill Borgeson, MSW
Program Manager, Kindle Family
Connections Casa Pacifica
Camarillo, California 93012

How hopeless would you feel being alone in a country where there are so many ways to connect with people, but still be unable to reach your own family? Where or how do you start? This child was fortunate to be in the care of Casa Pacifica and people who are so dedicated to helping children.

Jill has a special place in my heart. She was the head of one of the first agencies who came to us with family finding cases. Jill is passionate about helping the children under her care. I have always seen her as a role model for other supervisors in foster care. It has been an honor and a privilege to work with Jill to reunite the foster children under her care with their families.

*   *   *

Dear Mr. Villasana,

On behalf of CASA of Travis County, I sincerely thank you for the continued assistance and family finding expertise provided by Forever Homes for Foster Kids. Most recently, Forever Homes located a maternal grandmother of a 13-year-old boy who is currently in foster care. Our greatest challenge for this case has been identifying and contacting family members who we know live in Mexico, as well as family members who are undocumented in the U.S.

We are completely open to looking outside the country as well as working with undocumented relatives, but do not have the expertise to locate the relatives. Because of your considerable and dedicated research, we were able to establish direct contact with this child's family in Mexico, as well as identify relatives in the U.S.

The CASA volunteer used the information Forever Homes provided to contact the maternal grandmother the child had always spoke fondly about in the past. We found that the child once lived with the grandmother in Mexico. The grandmother was very concerned about the child and requested to begin contact. I must emphasize that, at the time, the boy had no contact with his family. The grandmother was also able to give the CASA volunteer information regarding her brother (maternal great-uncle), who lives in Texas, who may be able to provide support to the child.

The CASA volunteer is currently in the process of contacting the maternal great-uncle to explore the possibility of a relationship with the child. The child advocates are in the process of creating a plan to begin the process of engagement with the grandmother. This is great news for a case with little hope.

I am confident CASA of Travis County would not have found this information without the help of Forever Homes for Foster Kids. Again, please accept our most sincere appreciation for the work your organization provides to our CASA children.

Regards,

Anjuli (A.J.) Barak
Family Finding Specialist
CASA of Travis County
Austin, Texas 78752

How many pivotal moments have you had in your life? Sometimes you don't recognize them for what they are at the time. But, looking back you can see how, if one circumstance had been different or if you had made a different choice, the entire trajectory of your life would have been altered. As humans, we are so fascinated by "what if" scenarios that we create stories, movies, and even cinematic universes from the concept. We deal with it every day when we work with family reunification.

It is not uncommon for our international family finding to uncover a previously unknown relative of a foster child. Sometimes it's these distant relatives who step up and take in a child or who know of other relatives in the U.S. who will do so.

A child can experience several horrible outcomes than just spending years alone in the foster care system. Many who age out end up homeless. Right now cities across the U.S. are making being homeless a crime. An 18-year-old foster teen could be out of their foster home this afternoon, homeless tonight, and picked up and locked up in jail in a few days. They can't go to class or do their homework.

Once released, this teen has no place to live so they are panhandling... or worse. They could get beaten or killed because they are sleeping on the street. If relatives are found, they may step up and take the kid in before any of this happens. It's like a multiverse of possibilities within a single life that touches others. It creates a ripple effect, impacting communities of all sizes.

So many possibilities, many of them terrible, but one single outcome completely changes this foster child's life because of family finding. A child is better off when they are with family because they feel a sense of love and belonging. Finding relatives and getting a child back to their family is the very best outcome that every child deserves to enjoy.

The family reunification process influences the early pivotal moments in this foster child's life. Such moments are a formative part of the kid's life story and identity. Family reunification becomes that crystalized moment when the child realized people cared enough to help them... The memory of being reconnected with a loving family. And it is an opportunity to change the course of their life, helping them to have the stability and support they need to grow into happy, healthy, contributing members of their community.

*   *   *

Mr. Villasana,

I want to thank your organization, Forever Homes for Foster Kids, for its specialized family finding service. We were able to find family members for one of our foster children. We get cases where biological parents and maternal and paternal relatives need to be located and notified about their child who is with a foster care agency. We are very skilled at finding relatives in the U.S., but we had hit a dead end with this case because we were told that the father was living in Mexico and we did not have any identifying information to help us locate him. We do not currently have the resources in place to look for family members outside the country.

Seneca Family of Agencies lifelong Connections Permanency team works in collaboration with Sonoma County Department of Family, Youth & Children to reconnect foster youth with maternal and paternal family members that they may have lost touch with throughout their transitions within the foster care system.

Fortunately, Forever Homes for Foster Kids provided us with an important evaluation of our case data and then performed diligence to find the youth's father and his relatives. The end result is that we were able to find the youth's biological father, paternal grandfather, and paternal aunts and uncles currently living in Mexico. As a result, the youth now has his family members' contact information and is beginning to build a relationship with paternal family members that he otherwise may not have had.

Your organization sparked these results and was successful in its efforts. We also appreciate that we will be receiving important documents that we can provide to the foster child.

Again, accept our sincere gratitude. Forever Homes for Foster Kids provided an important service to agencies such as ours and the children we serve.

Kelly Chiaroni
Permanency Clinician
Seneca Family of Agencies
San Leandro, California 94578

Can you imagine what it would be like to grow up without any connection to people who look or act like you? How would you feel getting an assignment from school asking you to describe your connections to your family? Did your artistic talent come from your great-grandfather? Does your mother have the same gap between her two front teeth? Can someone explain why a specific smell from your childhood always makes you feel safe and warm?

A child wants to know which family members they take after. Many kids don't feel whole if they don't know their family.

Sometimes challenges within a single parent home result in a child being placed in foster care. Some of these parents have said that caring for their child was simply too much for them to handle. These kids may have little or no knowledge about the other birth parent and their relatives. Fortunately, this child went from not having a father to having a dad, paternal grandparents and many other relatives.

Family finding gives a child that sense of knowing who they are and where they come from. It's a basic longing and desire that makes a person feel whole, not as though something vital is missing. A child who feels connected to all their family has confidence and feels safe. Helping to give these qualities to a child is important and worth the investment.

*   *   *

Dear Forever Homes for Foster Kids,

On behalf of Barron County Department of Health and Human Services, I want to thank you for the work your agency did in completing a level one search for one of our identified clients known to be deported to Mexico several years ago. Your agency provided this service to this Department pro bono. Additionally, your response to my inquiry was immediate and the timeliness of the report exceeded my expectations.

As a result of your work our department was able to proceed in terminating parental rights on two children so that they could be adopted with their younger two siblings by their foster family. These two children were abandoned in foster care, and the legal requirement of proper notice caused multiple adjournments through the Court system. Prior to your involvement, the Court process was delayed for over one year. Within 30 days of your agency involvement, the court case is resolved. As a result of Forever Homes for Foster Kids, these children were given the gift of permanency.

I have a high regard for the work that your agency does for children and families. I will most definitely refer other colleagues needing similar services to your agency.

Thank you again for the exceptional work you have done. You should be very proud of the work you do as an agency.

Respectfully,

Jessica T. Wager
Social Worker III
Barron County Department of Health and Human Services
Barron Wisconsin 54812

Have you ever felt like second-best? Have you ever wondered how fortune smiled so easily on someone so much like you, while you felt like you struggled for basic survival? Imagine two older siblings being foster kids while their two younger siblings were adopted and could call their new parents mom and dad. The older two may have had some emotional resentment and hurt feelings, questioning why they couldn't be together. There is always the possibility that an older sibling in foster care will age out leaving younger siblings on their alone. Many foster kids cry or have nightmares because they are so afraid that their older sister or brother is out there somewhere being hurt.

Foster care is at its best when brothers and sisters are able to leave the system and grow up together in a safe, loving home. This case was special because almost everyone had expected further delays in completing the adoption. Family finding solved all of this because all four siblings have now been adopted by their former foster parents. These kids don't have to fear being separated. They have loving parents. They have family. They belong.

Family isn't always about biology. It's about love and caring. The power of finding relatives can mean a child will be with their mom or dad or a new, more loving, caring family. It gives children closure and the confidence to know someone cared enough to search and help them find their family, in whatever form will best support them.

Chapter Fourteen

Fixing Foster Care
For All Children

At the time of this writing, thousands of children are crossing into the United States from Latin America. The federal government is struggling to find a way to stem this tide of children coming into the country, many without a parent. As someone who is from a business background, I'm always looking for solutions. One of the reasons Forever Homes has been so successful in locating relatives internationally is that we look at how we can make this happen. There are definitive actions that government agencies, politicians and you can take to make positive changes in foster care for the children in the system.

As with any social topic, there are people who will criticize the government. This is not to say that the criticism is without merit. After decades of having a foster care system in this country, it is astounding how vastly different services are for children depending on the state and even the county in which these children live. But it is time to focus on solutions because every day children are being abused at home or killed while others are coming into the foster care system and are also being abused or killed. Children are being used as pawns by angry or violent spouses or partners, taking these children and killing them to get back at someone else, whether it's a spouse, former partner or relative.

Let's look at some action steps that government agencies and politicians can take to make positive changes for foster children.

Every foster care agency needs to have a set budget. These agencies must be able to count on a certain amount of money year in and year out so that they can plan ahead and not have to cut back on services. An April 2022 Southern Illinoisan article covered the horrific results of slashing the state's foster care budget.

> *"Tragically, when former Gov. Rauner decimated social services, we were warned that it would be much easier to lose the 500 beds he destroyed than to recreate them again. Advocates warned that these services weren't like a light switch that could be turned on and off with ease."*

Foster children are not products or services. Their needs cannot be delayed no more so than your breaking your arm and being able to wait until next week to see the doctor. The article continues by revealing that even though *"there are empty beds at existing group homes and residential facilities, they are not appropriately staffed."*

When foster care agencies don't have enough funding, it's always the children who suffer. They end up sleeping in office hallways, the break room or even a closet. Worse, pressured caseworkers have placed kids in foster and group homes with questionable safety. This bending of the rules has resulted in foster children being physically and sexually abused. Budgets across the country have been slashed to such an extent that it may take several years before every agency is functioning at a level where the immediate needs of each foster child are being met.

Bottom line: Every foster care agency needs to have a budget that adequately allows for the needs of the children both this year and the following year. Otherwise, good management and financial stewardship end up getting "rewarded" by having their budget cut for the next year. It's time for the United States to stop acting like it's a third world country and start taking care of its children.

The federal government may also need to establish policy so that each state has adequate funds for foster care. Too many state governors don't look kindly on impoverished children. Cutting foster care budgets is a nasty, ruthless way to win political points. The welfare of this country's children should not be used as a political bargaining chip. Our children deserve much better.

Adequate budgets will also allow for much of the following:

- Training, training and more training! Sales teams have training meetings almost daily. Certain professions require industry members to have annual training to maintain their licenses or certificates.

  Members of the military are always training for something. Nobody questions the need for training or the associated costs. Yet somehow, there is no formal certification or ongoing training for caseworkers. This isn't to say that in some counties or even in some states that no training occurs because it does, but the foster care system has no set national standards at least when it comes to family finding. Pretty much anything goes. This lack of training also extends to staff who conduct the intake process of gathering critical information about the child, the parent, and the family. I know this because when we receive a case and the only specific address listed is the name of a country, such as El Salvador, it's very obvious that the person doing the intake did not do a very good job.

Even if one person is highly skilled, their ability to function at a peak level is often limited because of poor communication. Today's jobs require continuous training and education so that people are able to function and provide quality service. Leading corporations understand this requirement and have built into their operation time for training at all levels of the company. This is done so that these companies can provide the best customer service resulting in the most profit. Foster care, of course, is not a corporation with the goal of making the most money, but every foster child deserves to have staff that is trained and knowledgeable in the best ways to serve them.

- Realistic caseloads need to be established at the national level. Foster care caseworkers often have incredible caseloads that are impossible for one person to manage. We're not working with an industry where a machine can come in to do the job. Technology can be a part of improving the foster care system, but this system is built on people. States need to stop treating foster care as if it's a sponge where caseworkers can absorb any number of children and each child will miraculously receive the quality care they deserve. It is simply impossible to provide quality service to each child when there are not enough caseworkers to deal with them. It is also unfair to caseworkers to expect them to do more than is possible. This is not a "boo hoo" situation. Kids are dying, and a lot of these deaths as well as abuses are preventable.

Many problems that foster kids experience are due to caseworkers not having enough time to visit each home to ensure that the children are living in a safe environment. Time and again, children who have been flagged to be monitored by Child Welfare are removed from their parents only after a crisis or incident that prompted a visit by the police or a caseworker. It's only during these visits that authorities are able to see the terrible squalor that a child or the children have been living in or evidence pointing to abuse or starvation.

The same challenges arise when a child is placed in foster care. Too often a caseworker simply can't get to every home monthly to ensure that each child is being cared for properly. How bad can this lapse get?

An October 2016 article by the San Antonio Current revealed that: *"close to 1,000 of Texas' most at-risk children in foster care have been denied crucial daily check-ins by the state's Child Protective Services... This number only represents children at 'immediate risk of physical or sexual abuse' — in total, the state has let nearly 5,000 children suspected of abuse go without necessary face-to-face visits."*

The reason I keep mentioning solutions at the national level is that this country's foster care system is fragmented among the more than 3,000 counties. California alone has 58 counties. As one family attorney commented, *"That's 58 counties with each one believing they are their own universe."* To any person who dislikes the idea of the federal government encroaching on state and county activities, I will simply say that the present model is not functioning well. Change is needed, and that change needs to happen now!

- National levels of service need to be established for children. It's shocking that in 2022 there are counties, even states, that do not have a formal training program on sex trafficking. Such training is so important because thousands of foster kids run away each year, and during their time on the street, many kids become involved with sex trafficking. They need therapy but rarely get it. Homeless people, including former foster kids, are often treated worse than animals. Injure a dog, and you may get six months in jail. Shoot a homeless person with a pellet gun, and you might just get a stern warning.

- Family finding must be one of the critical pillars of the foster care system. It is now pretty much an ad hoc program left up to the whims of each county about whether it wants to have a family finding program and, if so, how competent a program. Many counties have either no family finding program in place or it is in its infancy.

Our nonprofit did market research in 2014 about the popularity and extent of family finding. We called the main office of many California county foster care agencies asking to be connected to their family finding department. Many receptionists did not understand what we were saying. They simply had no idea what family finding was, and several had no idea their county had a family finding department. In some cases, they were correct. For other counties, family finding was relegated to such a small component of the foster care system that only one or two people were handling it for all the children under their care. A handful of counties had a contract with just one person to perform these duties. If this person is not educated about family finding internationally, does not speak or read Spanish, then Latino foster children in that county are simply out of luck. More pointedly, those children are at high risk of having their civil rights violated. The lack of performing family finding for a foster child is a violation of state and federal laws.

- Congress needs to put some accountability into the Fostering Connections Act, meaning throwing out the guidelines and putting in regulations. If the states want federal dollars for family finding, they need to establish a process that can be audited. Not putting enough funds into family finding per child means the federal government doesn't just hold back those funds. Make it hurt by holding back other federal funds. You may be thinking, "That just hurts the children." In extreme cases it would for the short term, but that's already happening. When elections come around, people can vote in better politicians who will ensure that their state or county gets every dollar possible by meeting federal requirements.

Not possible? Not the way things work? It is time for adults to stop dragging their lip on the ground, hiding in the corner and saying, "Nothing will change. It's just the way things work." Screw that! People across the country want to ban books based on the perceptions of a few. Do you think people four years ago saw that one coming? What it means is that once people get emotional enough about a particular topic, things can change very quickly whether for the good or the bad. I hope that people get riled up enough about the terrible defects in the foster care system that they will want to do something about it.

The 2020 article by Barbara H. Chaiyachati, MD, PhD, published in JAMA (Journal of the American Medical Association) Pediatrics, revealed that *"children in the foster care system are 42% more likely to die than children in the general population."*

The 2019 Adoption and Foster Care Analysis and Reporting System (AFCARS) disclosed that 385 children died while in foster care. To put this into perspective, 608 children twelve and younger died in vehicle crashes that same year, and about 400 children died from Covid-19 by July 2021. Dr. Rochelle Walensky, director of the U.S. Center for Disease Control and Prevention (CDC), told Sen. Roger Marshall during a briefing, *"Children are not supposed to die."* She got that right.

It's time to say, *"Hundreds of children dying in foster care each year has to stop!"*

Adequate oversight must be part of the evolution of foster care if there is ever to be any hope that children in this country will be treated humanely and be afforded opportunities to get a good education and have a healthy living free from abuse and neglect. Existing oversight agencies are simply not doing the best job possible. While deficiencies impact all foster children, Latino kids are once again severely discriminated by foster care agencies across the country.

Case in point is the state of Illinois' Department of Children and Family Services. In their 2019 article by Melissa Sanchez and Duaa Eldeib, ProPublica Illinois cast a critically harsh light on the immense failings of the foster care system for Latinos.

> *"For more than 40 years, the Illinois Department of Children and Family Services has been under a federal court order to place the children of Spanish speaking, Latino parents in foster homes where that language is spoken. This order, known as the Burgos consent decree, has the power to benefit thousands of families in a state with one of the country's largest Spanish-speaking populations. But a ProPublica Illinois investigation has found that DCFS [Department of Children and Family Services] has repeatedly failed in its obligations to help Spanish-speaking families."*

The article showcased one Latino father, Matias, who couldn't continue to talk with his one-year-old boy. He had been placed with a foster family who spoke Slovak. Within a year, the boy only spoke Slovak.

Did matters get better? A 2021 follow up report revealed horrific failings for Latino family and children.

> Charles Golbert, the Cook County public guardian, *"grew worried that Illinois' child welfare agency once again was failing the Spanish-speaking families*

whose children were in its care. For 10 months, lawyers from his office counted the number of new cases that involved Spanish-speaking families. Then the staffers checked how many of those families' files included a critical document, a 'language determination form,' that determines whether the Illinois Department of Children and Family Services must provide them services in Spanish, as required by a federal court order. Of the 80 or so cases the lawyers identified, Golbert said not one included the so-called language determination form."

Once again, the Illinois agency violated a federal court order and discriminated against Latino foster children and their families despite the involvement of a federal court. When is someone going to go to jail for these violations of civil rights?!

Most, if not all, states have an oversight committee supposedly looking after the best interest of the state's foster children. However, some of these committees are helping with the one hand and taking away with the other. Years ago, I spoke to one of the top officials at the California Foster Caregiver Policy and Support Unit in Sacramento, California about the need for county foster care agencies to search for a foster child's relatives even if those family members were living in Mexico. The official agreed wholeheartedly that family finding should extend at least to Mexico during my first call with her. However, during a follow up call this oversight committee official started offering excuses as to how a county could legally avoid performing family finding outside the U.S. for a child's relatives including a parent. Instead of looking for ways to ensure that each California foster child received equal treatment, this official was busy looking for loopholes.

Fortunately, oversight can also come from the courts. It is incredibly important that judges are informed about family finding. If a judge lacks the understanding that a child's relatives in Latin America can be located, it is likely the judge will not insist or even ask if such family finding efforts have been made on behalf of the child. On the other hand, several cases have been presented to us because the presiding judge thought the foster care agency had not made a best effort to perform family finding on behalf of a foster child. Over the last several years, some judges have begun to demand that agencies exert more effort to locate relatives in Latin America. Without this attention, many more children will suffer years of isolation from their families.

One Latin American case that we handled involved a foster child under the care of a county agency in North Carolina. The judge had requested family finding in Mexico for the foster teen. The only time the social worker would take quick action on our requests for documents and information was when he was scheduled to go before the family court judge who demanded updates about the family finding progress. Without the pressure the judge placed on this social worker, it's very likely that the case would have dragged on for more than a year. Instead, the case was closed within a few months, the child was adopted by a loving family and the county saved thousands of dollars in foster care costs.

However, many judges in this country are not knowledgeable about family finding. Until every judge in the country receives training, it's unlikely that the courts will be able to provide adequate oversight for foster children.

A minimal standard must be set for every foster care agency. The foster care industry is one that is sorely lacking in innovation and creativity. The industry as a whole fails to take advantage of the millions of cases it handles and for people within the foster care system to learn from these cases. Foster care can very often be reactive rather than proactive. In those cases where an oversight committee does identify issues that negatively affect the lives and safety of children, it usually ends up that these issues have been going on for years, if not decades.

Some companies have a checklist of the most important aspects of a job. This checklist can include areas that are the most critical to success. While these checklists may not include everything, they can at least include items that, if checked off, indicate that more investigation is warranted. If a child responds that they have been involved with sex trafficking, then that child needs and deserves more psychological attention.

Much more care needs to be taken about how adults communicate with children. Children need to feel heard, and part of that hearing is for teachers, administrators, caseworkers, police officers and other adults to truly listen and at least consider that the child may be telling the truth. Children who are at risk continue to suffer in silence because of a lack of systems and procedures and the poor treatment they receive when they share about a terrible situation with an adult.

These are just the fundamentals of foster care. We haven't even started talking about the needs involving children who are from different ethnicities and cultures or children with physical or mental issues. These children need even more care. The caseworkers who work with them need more training to properly understand what has happened to these kids and the best recourse to ensure that each child receives the help that they must have.

Even though a lot of these ideas have been directed at government agencies, it is simply unrealistic to expect that the government is going to be able to adequately meet every challenge for each child. Nonprofits will always be a significant part of the foster care landscape as they are with others.

A few years ago, National Public Radio (NPR) aired a segment concerning the ongoing lack of service that veterans were receiving from the Veterans Administration (VA). A couple of nonprofits were highlighted about the services they provided to veterans. One nonprofit worked to find wheelchairs for veterans who needed help to get around and be independent.

Despite ongoing and continued interest on the part of elected leaders to ensure that U.S. veterans get the proper medical and psychological treatment and/or products they need to lead the best life possible, the VA still came up short. A shockingly truthful moment during the episode came when a high-level VA official said that without the help of nonprofits, the administration would not be able to provide veterans with the care they needed. This official understood that the government alone cannot step up and provide for every contingency and situation and said so. Gaps in the VA's service exist and will most likely remain. Without nonprofits coming forward and filling these gaps, veterans would suffer.

The same is true of foster care and the children in the system. State and county agencies will never be able to completely provide a safe and loving environment for these children. Nonprofits have an ability to focus attention and effort on an industry's deficiencies. Nonprofits are and will continue to be a vital component of the foster care system working together to ensure the best outcome for each child.

Speaking of nonprofits and government agencies, here's some sobering and sage advice to both—**Learn to collaborate!** One of the most important lessons I learned from business and the military was the power of teamwork, people working together so that everyone benefits. Too many nonprofits act like Gollum from "Lord of the Rings" because they desperately try to hold on to their "precious" meaning their procedures or corporate supporters. I can't tell you how many nonprofits and government agencies have shut down talks that would have provided new and better services to both foster and immigrant children because they fear collaboration. Both types of organizations need to learn how to take better advantage of opportunities that will give more foster children better outcomes while moving each agency closer to achieving their mission and vision.

Now here are some ways that you can help a foster child. Volunteer some time each month to help a nonprofit that is involved with foster children. Most likely there is a nonprofit already serving some aspect of foster care where you could give your time and feel very rewarded. Every dollar that is not spent on staff is a dollar that can go towards helping a foster child. Nonprofits operate just like any business. They need help in all areas of their operation. If you can do graphics, social media, audio and visual work, office administration, fundraising, event planning, data entry, grant writing or research, there's a nonprofit waiting and wanting your help. If you have great passion and a desire to see changes in the foster care system, then look for opportunities and nonprofits where you can be the one to drive and promote new legislation that will benefit children.

You can be part of the solution by becoming a CASA (Court Appointed Special Advocate) volunteer. This allows you to become the voice in court for a foster child. Once trained, you will spend ten to fifteen hours a month being the voice for a foster child in court. As a CASA volunteer, you can push for quality family finding and help ensure relatives are found and notified. The emotional rewards of helping a child can be richly satisfying.

If you don't have a lot of time to give, find a nonprofit and support them through their social media. We have dedicated followers who comment almost daily on our Facebook and Instagram posts. People who want to make a difference start Facebook fundraisers. If you don't have any time, then give generously to a nonprofit.

Donations are an excellent way to help a foster kid, and it's not always with money. Kids and teens collect backpacks, clothes and toys for foster children. Many professionals help a nonprofit by donating products or providing services such as accounting, marketing, web design, publicity advice and much more. Some people donate their old car, and others donate simply when they buy something on Amazon.

You just read many ways to help a nonprofit, and most are ways that you and others can help Forever Homes. Every minute and dollar that we are not spending on data entry, social media, etc. is time and money that is devoted to reuniting a child with family. Remember that we provide our services free of charge. The more donations we receive, the more children we can help.

We both know that nothing I have written here is new. A business that doesn't have enough cash flow goes out of business. Foster care budgets that are far too small for the number of children coming in is a recipe for disaster that is happening all across the country. Too many students in the classroom means that some will not get enough needed attention. Too many kids assigned to a caseworker means one or more foster kids are now at risk. It's time for our politicians to push laws that ensure every child's civil rights are respected. Government agencies and nonprofits need to learn to play nicer with each other. Finally, every kid, teen and adult has the ability the help a foster child have a better, brighter future. Now is the time to make things happen.

"Each of us, as citizens, has a role to play
in creating a better world for
our children."

Nelson Mandela

Discover how you can volunteer or raise donations to help a foster child. Go to:
www.ForeverHomesforFosterKids.org/help-foster-kid

Chapter Fifteen

Today's Hope for
Better Foster Care Tomorrow

I want to celebrate five groups of people and organizations that give hope to hundreds of thousands of foster children each and every year. No matter how broken the foster care system is, there is a lot that works well and knowing this often gives inspiration that we can do better for these children.

Foster Parents: When you hear about foster parents in the news, it's often a story about how something has gone very badly. Not often enough do people hear about the thousands of selfless foster parents who are caring for the children who enter the foster care system. These adults who are critically important to the wellbeing of children placed in foster care normally go through a rigorous process to become licensed foster parents.

While family finding efforts are being executed, children can be placed morning, noon or night with a couple or single adult. Foster parents have signed on to take a child into their home who may have serious anger issues, emotional trauma that hasn't been properly treated or other tendencies such as urinating on the couch, beating other kids, breaking furniture or stealing food and hiding it under their bed. Foster kids may not allow a foster parent to hug them or treat them with affection. Yet thousands of adults are willing to take in a child, sometimes as many as five at a time, and do their best to care for and love the child.

Jen Lilley, actress, foster and adoptive mom and child advocate, writes about being a foster mom.

> *"Foster parenting is hard, I think I cried every single day; but those tears watered seeds of love, empathy, compassion, and grace deep in my heart I had no idea were there. Foster care is first and foremost about healing the children in your care and hopefully alleviating at least some of the absolute turmoil they're going through. But what a beautiful reward as the caregiver to experience more empathy and compassion for others as a result of foster care's brokenness. Don't believe the excuse 'I could never be a foster parent because I'd get too attached.' My friend, that makes you the perfect foster parent. These precious children need us and our attachment more than we need to protect our hearts, and I truly believe in the end, your heart will benefit as much as the children in your care."*

Foster parents such as Jen Lilley know that at any minute the child they have come to love may be taken from them either to go to another foster home or back to their birth parent or guardian. That's sacrifice. That's true love. That's being a hero, and children certainly need more heroes like caring foster parents in this world because there are never enough.

Caseworkers: Where to start? Being a caseworker has to be a labor of love. Many people dislike and some despise caseworkers because of bad, even terrible outcomes that have happened to kids and families. But once again, overlooked are the thousands of adults who are dedicated and doing their best on behalf of a foster child.

We have been privileged to work with many outstanding caseworkers such as Jill Borgeson with Ventura County Children and Family Services who have gone over and beyond to perform exhaustive family finding to locate parents and other adult relatives. Because of the dedication of these caseworkers, more foster children have been placed with an aunt or grandparent instead of being left to spend years alone in the system.

Many caseworkers are often handling an impossible number of children. Burnout for these professionals is very high. They have to endure the emotional toll of the work along with management that often does not give them the tools, training or support to do a competent job. Caseworkers often go to homes without any police support and may be putting their health or life on the line to ensure that a child is safe from harm. Some caseworkers are verbally or physically attacked by a parent or guardian. A few have lost their lives. Yet people keep joining the ranks of caseworkers to do their best because most care about children and want to help give a child a better future. These adults deserve much more respect than they get from the public.

Judges: These men and women can and often are a primary source of motivation for foster care agencies. Judges can insist on a more extensive family finding effort. We handled a case in Florida in which the foster care agency was instructed by the judge to do a more thorough family finding. The staff in that particular county lacked the resources to meet the demands of this judge so the caseworker contacted our nonprofit. Our organization succeeded in locating the foster child's mother and father. The judge in this case helped to bring about a happy outcome for the youth by insisting on a better level of performance from the agency. Family finding works best when all parties involved work together. Judge (Ret.) Leonard P. Edwards, one of the judges I admire, once said, *"It's my dream that the expanded use of family finding will literally dry up the foster care system."* We need more judges to help make this dream a reality for foster kids.

Nonprofits: Thousands of charitable organizations work to help foster children. A nonprofit exists for virtually every aspect of foster care. Some create a welcome kit for a child who comes into foster care with just a diaper. Others collect toys, blankets, books and backpacks so each foster kid has something that's theirs. Some nonprofits have a mission to ensure that foster kids graduate high school and, if they want, enter and stay in college. Other charities have sprung up to provide needed transitional services to foster kids who would otherwise be on the streets alone with no guidance or support while still in their teens. Some engage in family finding and take to heart the mandate of the FCA to locate a foster child's adult relatives.

One organization that goes the extra mile is Turning Points for Children in Philadelphia. We have handled several of their cases because the organization wants to be thorough in its family finding efforts. They understand that quality family finding often results in foster children being placed with relatives or adopted. Either way, these children are with loving people and not spending years in a government institution. The beautiful thing about nonprofits is that they can see local problems clearly and create practical, economical solutions that solve important issues like reuniting a foster child with family.

Supporters:

Millions of individuals and businesses support efforts to improve the lives of foster children. Some are large companies such as Mattress Firm, the nation's leading specialty bedding retailer. Year round, it promotes the collection of clothing, shoes and school supplies for needy foster kids. The Dave Thomas Foundation for Adoption focuses on getting foster children adopted. There are business leaders such as Facebook mavin Gia Heller, CEO of the Social Media Masters, who was a foster parent and is a huge supporter of foster youths. Other supporters include artists who generously provide artwork that helps to increase donations.

Then there are those wonderful, big-hearted individuals who support foster kids through donations, fundraisers, volunteer work and advocacy. The contributions from these businesses and individuals allow nonprofits such as Forever Homes for Foster Kids to provide services that directly help foster children.

If you consider the foster care system to be broken, and many politicians, judges and youth experts say that it is, then just imagine how much more difficult life would be for foster kids without these individuals and organizations. We truly owe them a huge debt of gratitude.

Creating a Better Future for Foster Kids, Together:

The combined work of all these groups of people can, and does, change the course of many children's lives. We cannot overstate the impact on each kid we help. And yet, there are still over 423,900 children in foster care. Some of them will simply disappear from their foster homes. Others will be forced out onto the streets where, without support, they will be left to survive by whatever means they can. Many of these kids will become sex trafficking victims.

Think about the hundreds of thousands of foster children who have no control over their fates. They are separated from their parents and families and quite likely traumatized by their surroundings. Instead of spending time living their lives and being loved by their families, these children are utterly alone. These children desperately need not only a voice but concerted, deliberate action on their part. But these abandoned kids have no voice or representation in government... Who will be their champion?

I have this cynical optimism that the United States government might feel a moral imperative to act. Perhaps someone else entirely might step up and start to do things properly to get more immigrant and foster children reunited with their families... But these kids can't afford for their futures to be left to chance. Without action, hope will not change their lives.

It is our collective responsibility to support and raise these children through adulthood. To help them grow to become happy, healthy, and contributing adults in our society, we must nurture them. As individuals, it can be difficult to know where to start when so many of the problems are on a national scale. But one of the most important actions you can take to influence greater changes and help create a better foster care system is using your voice on their behalf.

Your advocacy can start with demanding that better family finding services are provided by your local state and county agencies. It's the right thing to do, and it's the law. Localized, public accountability can force the most reluctant officials and failing institutions to follow their mandate.

The foster children of this country deserve, and are owed, the very best we can give – a fighting chance for a life of their own. Together, we can transform the foster care system and create one that offers these children the very best futures possible. We can support them into adulthood, preparing them to join us in building stronger, healthier communities where they are welcomed and wanted.

It's time to do what's right and just for children.

Chapter Sixteen

Why Help a Foster Child

You're busy. You have a life. You have responsibilities, probably people who count on you. What good will it do to help just one foster child?

A lot.

Imagine if Simone Biles' grandfather hadn't taken her from foster care and adopted her. Would she be the GOAT (Greatest Of All Times) of gymnastics with enough Olympic gold to start her own bank and receive the Presidential Medal of Freedom? Probably not. Becoming an Olympic athlete takes focus and support. A stable home life plays a crucial part in reaching that level of excellence. Have an Apple phone or watch? You probably wouldn't if Steve Jobs hadn't been adopted into a loving, supportive family. What about Oprah, Michael Bay, Les Brown, Sylvester Stallone, Tiffany Haddish, Kristin Chenoweth — all of them foster children and/or adoptees — and, well, you get the idea.

Let's talk about you. At some point in your life, someone helped you out, picked you up, nudged you to take action. That person was thinking of you. They were focused on you, and whatever your story is, their caring about you made a positive difference.

When you contribute to the life of a child, no matter what or how, you are making a difference to that child. The difference could be a little girl getting to meet her father whom she hasn't seen in four years. It can be her father telling her that he's moving to where she is so that he can bring her home. It could be a girl who gets adopted by her grandparents and who then becomes this country's GOAT. It could simply be a little boy who gets adopted and now has an older brother and sister. You don't know who you will help, but you will flip a foster kid's world.

And when you do help, you join a special group of people who have opened their heart to an innocent child. Giving also gives you a warm glow without the caffeine or calories. Why help a foster child? You deserve to ride that wave of good feelings that only comes when you give and know that doing so will make a difference for a kid. Pizza may fill up your stomach but giving will stuff your soul.

Chapter Seventeen

How to Help a Foster Child

You can help move a foster child from being alone in a strange place to being reunited with loving, caring family members who will give this deserving child the permanent home they need.

Here's how.

- Follow us on Facebook at www.facebook.com/family findingmx. You can like our page and share our posts. Increasing awareness about foster children is very necessary.

- Do a fundraiser on Facebook to reunite a foster kid with family. It's super easy to set up at www.facebook. com/fund/familyfindingmx. Donations allow us to reunite a foster child with family.

- Volunteer a few hours each week to do research, call companies, organizations and politicians, research and do grant writing, supervise activities, create and run events, help with graphics, video and more.

- Donate when you buy through Amazon. Go to https://
  smile.amazon.com/ch/82-1256794. Once signed up, be
  sure to start your shopping at smile.amazon.com to
  donate and help a foster child or use the Amazon mobile
  app with AmazonSmile turned on within Settings.

- Donate your used car, boat or RV at www.careasy.org/
  nonprofit/forever-homes-for-foster-kids. Donating is
  easy, the pick-up is free, and your gift is tax-deductible.

- Become a sponsor. Support our work to reunite a
  foster child as an individual sponsor. Own a company?
  Become a corporate sponsor to give many foster children
  a forever home. If your company has an annual party
  or fundraiser, make Forever Homes the beneficiary.

For more information on ways to give to Forever Homes,
contact Scott Gobler at 760-690-3995 or at
giving@foreverhomesforfosterkids.org.

No matter what you choose, you can always help reunite
a foster child with family.

Sources

Introduction

U.S. Department of Health and Human Services, *Administration for Children and Families, Children's Bureau, Foster care statistics 2019*, <https://www.childwelfare.gov/pubpdfs/foster.pdf>.

U.S. Department of Health and Human Services, Administration for Children and Families, Administration for Children, Youth and Families, Children's Bureau 2020, *The AFCARS Report: Preliminary Estimates for FY2019 as of June 23, 2020 – No. 27*, <https://www.acf.hhs.gov/sites/default/files/documents/cb/afcarsreport27.pdf>.

The Annie E. Casey Foundation, KIDS COUNT Data Center, *Children in foster care by race and Hispanic origin in the United States*, <https://datacenter.kidscount.org/data/tables/ 6246-children-in-foster-care-by-race-and-hispanic-origin#detailed/1/any/false/ 1729,37,871,870,573,869,36,868,867,133/ 2638,2601,2600,2598,2603,2597,2602,1353/ 12992,12993>.

U.S. Department of Education 2016, *Foster Care Transition Toolkit*, <https://www2.ed.gov/about/inits/ed/foster-care/youth-transition-toolkit.pdf>.

Olsen, Darcy 2022, 'Foster care children are easy prey for predators: They disappear without a real search', *USA Today*, 24 February 2022, <https://www.usatoday.com/story/opinion/columnist/2022/02/24/children-disappear-foster-care-trafficking/6829115001/>.

Olsen, Darcy and Rebecca Masterson 2020, *Disappearing and Dying: Why 20,000 Kids disappear from foster care every year and how to end this crisis*, <https://2b997067-e6f0-44b9-abf5-69867df2e6d3.usrfiles.com/ugd/2b9970_059b8c1746d64a588d8616fc27c3678b.pdf>.

Fowler, Patrick J. et al. 2017, 'Homelessness and Aging Out of Foster Care: A National Comparison of Child Welfare-Involved Adolescents', *Children and Youth Services Review*, volume 77: 27-33, retrieved from <https://www.ncbi.nlm.nih.gov/pmc/articles/PMC5644395/#R10>.

Sarubbi, Molly, Emily Parker, and Brian A. Sponsler, ED.D. 2016, 'Strengthening Policies for Foster Youth Postsecondary Attainment', *Education Commission of the United States*, October 2016, <https://files.eric.ed.gov/fulltext/ED570481.pdf>.

Reagan, Michael 2015, 'Foster Kids Need Support After 18', *Newsmax*, 24 March 2015, <https://www.newsmax.com/reagan/foster-children-support-18/2015/03/24/id/634176/>.

Judge: Texas is to blame for foster care neglect, failures', *AP News*, 15 September 2021, <https://apnews.com/article/texas-foster-care-ea0829dbadbb68c871aa2b313b3916e5>.

Public Law 110-351, 110th Congress, 122 State 3949, 7 October 2008, <https://dokumen.tips/ documents/

public-law-110a351-110th-congress-an-act-public-law-
110a351aoct-7-2008-122.html>.

Chapter Two

U.S. Department of Health and Human Services Office
of the Inspector General 2019, 'Separated Children
Placed in Office of Refugee Resettlement Care', *HHS OIG
Brief OEI-BL-18-00511*, <https://oig.hhs.gov/oei/reports/
oei-BL-18-00511.pdf>.

Chapter Three

Esquival, Paloma Esmeralda Bermudez, and Nina
Agrawal 2018, 'Inside the California facilities holding children
separated from their parents at the border', *Los Angeles
Times*, 23 June 2018, <https://www.latimes.com/local/
la-me-detained-in-la-20180622-story.html>.

Gerstein, Josh and Ted Hesson 2018, 'Federal
judge orders Trump administration to reunite
migrant families', *Politico*, 26 June 2018,
<https://www.politico.com/story/2018/06/26/
judge-orders-trump-reunite-migrant-families-678809>.

Bermudez, Esmeralda 2018, 'Children separated from
parents arrive in L.A., but frustrated community gets few
answers', *Los Angeles Times*, 21 June 2018, <https://
www.latimes.com/local/california/la-me-ln-separated-
kids-la-20180620-story.html>.

Ms. L. v. U.S. Immigration and Customs Enforcement et
al, No. 3:2018cv00428 - Document 71 (S.D. Cal. 2018),
<https://law.justia.com/cases/federal/district courts/
california/casdce/3:2018cv00428/564097/71/>.

Chapter Four

U.S. Department of Health and Human Services Office of the Inspector General 2019, 'Separated Children Placed in Office of Refugee Resettlement Care', *HHS OIG Brief OEI-BL-18-00511*, <https://oig.hhs.gov/oei/reports/oei-BL-18-00511.pdf>.

Soboroff Jacob and Teaganne Finn 2022, 'White House supports permanent legal status for families separated at border', *NBC News*, 1 February 2022, <https://news.yahoo.com/white-house-supports-permanent-legal-223148172.html>.

Kight, Stef W. 2021, 'Exclusive: Government can't reach one-in-three released migrant kids', *Axios*, 1 September 2021, <https://www.axios.com/2021/09/01/migrant-children-biden-administration>.

Bostock, Bill 2021, 'Biden officials still can't find the parents of 337 children separated at the Mexico border by the Trump administration, court docs show', *Yahoo! News*, 12 August 2021, <https://www.yahoo.com/news/biden-officials-still-cant-parents-092612999.html>.

Spagat, Elliot 2019, 'Tally of children split at borders tops 5,400 in new count', *Yahoo! News*, 14 October 2019, <https://www.yahoo.com/news/tally-children-split-border-tops-015626897.html>.

Does USPS Lose Packages? (You'll be Surprised) 2022, <https://querysprout.com/does-usps-lose-packages/>.

The Annie E. Casey Foundation, *Youth in Transition (Aging Out)*, <https://www.aecf.org/topics/youth-in-transition>.

Center for Immigration Studies 2021, *Report: Government Can't Locate a Third of Alien Children It Released*, <https://cis.org/Arthur/Report-Government-Cant-Locate-Third-Alien-Children-It-Released>.

Chapter Five

Frolik, Cornelius 2022, 'Child removals have jumped in Montgomery County: Why is it happening?', *Dayton Daily News*, 15 May 2022, retrieved from <https://news.yahoo.com/child-removals-jumped-montgomery-county-141600635.html>.

Nueces County, TX Commissioners Court, Commissioner Chesney, <https://www.nuecesco.com /commissioners-court/commissioner-precinct-4/commissioner-chesney>.

Child and Family Services Agency (CFSA) 2010, *Quick Reference Guide: Notification to Relatives when a Child is removed from the Home*, <https://cfsa.dc.gov/sites/default/files/dc/sites/cfsa/publication/attachments/QRG%20-%20Removal%20Notification%20to%20Relatives%28H%29_0.pdf>.

Noonan, James 2011, 'County responds to child welfare report', *Napa Valley Register*, 16 September 2011, <https://napavalleyregister.com/news/local/county-responds-to-child-welfare-report/article_0a228e7a-e01c-11e0-9ad2-001cc4c002e0.html>.

Napa County Grand Jury 2010-2011, *Final Report on Napa County Child Welfare Services: Too Many Kids, Not Enough Help*, <https://www.napa.courts.ca.gov/sites/default/files/napa/default/2021-07/GJ-10-11-Child-Welfare.pdf>.

U.S. Department of Education 2016, *Foster Care Transition Toolkit*, <https://www2.ed.gov/about/inits/ed/foster-care/youth-transition-toolkit.pdf>.

Noe-Bustamante, Luis, Antonio Flores, and Sono Shah, 'Facts on Hispanics of Mexican Origin in the United States, 2017', *Pew Research Center*, <www.pewresearch.org/hispanic/fact-sheet/u-s-hispanics-facts-on-mexican-origin-latinos/>.

Budiman, Abby and Phillip Connor 2018, 'Migrants from Latin America and the Caribbean sent a record amount of money to their home countries in 2016', *Pew Research Center*, <www.pewresearch.org/fact-tank/2018/01/23/migrants-from-latin-america-and-the-caribbean-sent-a-record-amount-of-money-to-their-home-countries-in-2016/>.

Passel, Jeffrey S., Mark Hugo Lopez, and D'Vera Cohn 2022, 'U.S. Hispanic population continued its geographic spread in the 2010s', *Pew Research Center*, <www.pewresearch.org/fact-tank/2022/02/03/u-s-hispanic-population-continued-its-geographic-spread-in-the-2010s/>.

LaRowe, Lynn 2018, 'Appellate court sides with father from Mexico in child custody case', *Texarkana Gazette*, 10 November 2018, <https://www.texarkanagazette.com/news/2018/nov/10/appellate-court-sides-father-mexico-child-custody-/>.

Chapter Six

Jewett, Christina and Shefali Luthra 2018, 'Immigrant toddlers ordered to appear in court alone', *The Texas Tribune*, 27 June 2018,

<https://www.texastribune.org/2018/06/27/
immigrant-toddlers-ordered-appear-court-alone/>.

U.S. Department of Health and Human Service and
U.S. Department of Justice 2016, *Title VI Child Welfare
Guidance*, <https://www.justice.gov/opa/file/903996/
download>.

Galvan, Astrid 2018, 'Complaint: US officials coerced
migrants to sign documents', *AP News*, 23 August 2018,
<https://apnews.com/article/immigration-north-america-
us-news-ap-top-news-az-state-wire-e5eeb241115843eab
5a8716d6f76a263>.

Chapter Seven

Robinson, Jennifer 2021, 'Voces on PBS: American Exile',
KPBS, 12 November 2021, <https://www.kpbs.org/
news/2021/11/12/voces-on-pbs-american-exile>.

U.S. Citizenship and Immigration Services, *Consideration of
Deferred Action for Childhood Arrivals (DACA)*, <https://
www.uscis.gov/DACA>.

U.S. Citizenship and Immigration Services, *Approximate
Active DACA Recipients as of March 31, 2020*, <https://
www.uscis.gov/sites/default/files/document/data/
Approximate%20 Active%20DACA%20Receipts%20-%20
March%2031%2C%202020.pdf >.

Spagat, Elliot and Mark Sherman 2021, 'Biden rule to
shield 'Dreamers' seeks to bypass Congress', *ABC News*,
27 September 2021, <https://abcnews.go.com/Politics/
wireStory/ biden-administration-unveils-plan-young-
immigrants-80259932>.

U.S. Citizenship and Immigration Services, *Deferred Action for Childhood Arrivals: Response to January 2018 Preliminary Injunction*, <https://www.uscis.gov/archive/deferred-action-for-childhood-arrivals-response-to-january-2018-preliminary-injunction>.

NBC Universal, 'Biden administration says over 1,200 families who illegally crossed border still separated' [Video file], 2 February 2022, retrieved from <https://news.yahoo.com/biden-administration-says-over-1-180810449.html>.

Chapter Nine

United States Census Bureau, *QuickFacts Napa County, California*, <https://www.census.gov/quickfacts/napacounty california>.

Noonan, James 2011, 'County responds to child welfare report', *Napa Valley Register*, 16 September 2011, <https://napavalleyregister.com/news/local/county-responds-to-child-welfare-report/article_0a228e7a-e01c-11e0-9ad2-001cc4c002e0.html>.

Napa County Grand Jury 2010-2011, *Final Report on Napa County Child Welfare Services: Too Many Kids, Not Enough Help*, <https://www.napa.courts.ca.gov/sites/default/files/napa/default/2021-07/GJ-10-11-Child-Welfare.pdf>.

Jaffe, Logan 2019, '"How in 2019 Do We Not Have Enough Spanish-Speaking Caseworkers?"', *ProPublica*, 19 July 2019, <https://www.propublica.org/article/lawmakers-respond-dcfs-violations-burgos-order-spanish-speaking-services-to-spanish-speaking-families>.

Chapter Ten

Wiltz, Teresa 2015, 'States Tackle 'Aging Out' of Foster Care', *The PEW Charitable Trusts*, <https://www.pewtrusts.org/en/research-and-analysis/blogs/stateline/2015/3/25/states-tackle-aging-out-of-foster-care>.

Lee, Sidney 2016, 'Many Oklahomans, once in foster care, age out and are now homeless', *The Norman Transcript*, 18 April 2016, <https://www.normantranscript.com/news/many-oklahomans-once-in-foster-care-age-out-and-are-now-homeless/article_070609dc-ebf6-5ae7-843d-5f2e5c7b137c.html>.

Tennessee Faith Leaders 2022, 'Opinion: Faith leaders urge Gov. Bill Lee to veto homeless criminalization bill', *Tennessean*, 26 April 2022, <https://www.tennessean.com/story/ opinion/2022/04/26/homelessness-tennessee-gov-bill-lee-should-veto-harmful-bill/7445186001/>.

Sanders, Julia-Grace 2016, 'How Our Child-Welfare System Is Fostering the Homelessness Crisis', *Seattle Weekly*, 2 June 2016, <https://www.seattleweekly.com/news/how-our-child-welfare-systme-is-fostering-the-homelessness-crisis/>.

National Coalition for Child Protection Reform 2021, *The NCCPR Quick Read: Family Policing in America – An Overview*, <https://nccpr.org/the-nccpr-quick-read/>.

San Diego County Health and Human Services Agency, *Hepatitis A Outbreak in San Diego County is Officially Over*, <https://www.sandiegocounty.gov/content/sdc/

hhsa/programs/phs/community_epidemiology/dc/
Hepatitis_A.html>.

Baucum, Emily 2022, 'With families caught in middle, child welfare leader can't answer questions about training', *News 4 San Antonio*, 31 March 2022, <https://news4sanantonio.com/news/trouble-shooters/with-families-caught-in-middle-child-welfare-leader-cant-answer-questions-about-training>.

Brown, Jennifer 2021, 'The deadly consequences when kids run away from Colorado residential treatment centers', *The Colorado Sun*, 17 May 2021, <https://coloradosun.com/2021/ 05/17/children-teen-runaways-colorado-residential-centers/?utm_medium=email&utm_ source=govdelivery>.

Sewell, Abby 2012, 'Most L.A. County youths held for prostitution come from foster care', *Los Angeles Times*, 27 November 2012, <https://www.latimes.com/archives/la-xpm-2012-nov-27-la-me-1128-sex-trafficking-20121128-story.html>.

Chapter Eleven

Perry, Parker 2021, 'Mother sues Montgomery County, children services employees after child sexually abused', *Dayton Daily News*, 28 December 2021, <https://www.daytondailynews.com/crime/mother-sues-montgomery-county-children-services-employees-after-child-sexually-abused/ YLYZSXA7EZF5RGZCSFJTJUMNWM/>.

Sick, Chelsea 2021, 'Mother of 4 year old rape victim files lawsuit against Montgomery County Children Services', *Dayton 24/7 Now*, 28 December 2021, <https://

dayton247now.com/ news/local/mother-of-4-year-old-rape-victim-files-lawsuit-against-montgomery-county-children-services>.

Rodgers, Grant 2017, 'Starved teen found in diaper on linoleum floor, records reveal', *Des Moines Register*, 15 March 2017, <https://www.desmoinesregister.com/ story/news/ crime-and-courts/2017/03/15/teen-who-starved-death-found-diaper-linoleum-floor-court-documents-reveal/99213932/>.

Gurnon, Emily 2016, 'Childhood Trauma Effects Often Persist Into 50s and Beyond', *Next Avenue*, <https:// www.nextavenue.org/effects-childhood-trauma/>.

Chapter Twelve

Garrett, Robert 2017, 'Federal Judge Finds Texas has 'broken' foster care system, says she'll order changes', *The Dallas Morning News*, 17 December 2017, <https:// www.dallasnews.com/news/politics/2015/12/17/ federal-judge-finds-texas-has-broken-foster-care-system-says-she-ll-order-changes/>.

Texas Department of Family and Protective Services, *Foster Care Litigation*, <https://www.dfps.state.tx.us/ Child_Protection/Foster_Care/Litigation.asp>.

Zelinski, Andrea 2016, 'Judge beefs up plan to fix foster care', *Houston Chronicle*, 21 June 2016, <https://www. pressreader.com/usa/houston-chronicle/ 20160621/ 281487865643420>.

Zelinski, Andrea 2016, 'Judge doubles workload for team working on foster care overhaul', *Houston Chronicle*,

20 June 2016, <https://www.houstonchronicle.com/politics/texas/ article/Judge-doubles-workload-for-team-working-on-foster-8314096.php>.

Elizabeth, Erin 2019, 'Federal Judge in Texas Fines CPS $50K a Day for "Shameful" Foster Care: CPS has "Lied to me at almost Every Level"', *Erin Elizabeth's Health Nut News*, 10 November 2019, <https://www.healthnutnews.com/federal-judge-in-texas-fines-cps-50k-a-day-for-shameful-foster-care-cps-has-lied-to-me-at-almost-every-level/>.

Blakinger, Keri 2018, 'Texas judge orders rare $127,000 sanction against CPS after wrongful removal of children', *Chron*, 11 November 2018, <https://www.chron.com/news/houston-texas/houston/article/Texas-judge-orders-rare-127-000-sanction-against-13376803.php>.

Garrett, Robert 2018, 'To force Texas to improve its foster care system, judge exerts her authority in an aggressive plan', *The Dallas Morning News*, 21 November 2018, <https://www.dallasnews.com/news/politics/2018/11/21/to-force-texas-to-improve-its-foster-care-system-judge-exerts-her-authority-in-an-aggressive-plan/>.

Mizroch, Marissa 2022, 'Judge blasts state officials over conditions for foster kids sent out of state', *Spectrum News 1*, 20 January 2022, <https://spectrumlocalnews.com/tx/south-texas-el-paso/news/2022/01/21/judge-blasts-state-officials-over-conditions-for-texas-foster-kids-sent-out-of-state>.

The Annie E. Casey Foundation, KIDS COUNT Data Center, *Children in foster care (0-17) in Texas*, <https://datacenter.kidscount.org/data/

tables/3061-children-in-foster-care-0-17#detailed/2/
any/false/574,1729,37,871,870,573,869,36,868,867/
any/8263,8264>.

The Annie E. Casey Foundation 2016, 'Every Kid
Need a Family: A Message to Caseworkers' [Video
file], 14 October 2016, <https://www.youtube.com/
watch?v=Wc6Bq6gltGQ>.

Tiano, Sara 2021, 'Texas Lawmaker Wants to Give
Relative Caregivers a Raise', *The Imprint*, 17 March
2021, <https://imprintnews.org/child-welfare-2/texas-
lawmaker-wants-to-give-kin-caregivers-a-raise/52701>.

Chapter Fourteen

Downey, Jr., Ken 2020, 'Children in foster care 42%
more likely to die than children in general population',
Healio News, 24 April 2020, <https://www.healio.com/
news/pediatrics/ 20200424/ children-in-foster-care-42-
more-likely-to-die-than-children-in-general-population>.

U.S. Department of Health and Human Services,
Administration for Children and Families, Administration
for Children, Youth and Families, Children's Bureau
2020, *The AFCARS Report: Preliminary Estimates
for FY2019 as of June 23, 2020 – No. 27*, <https://
www.acf.hhs.gov/sites/default/files/documents/cb/
afcarsreport27.pdf>.

Centers for Disease Control and Prevention 2021,
*Transportation Safety: Child Passenger Safety – Get the
Facts*, <https://www.cdc.gov/transportationsafety/
child_passenger_safety/cps-factsheet.html>.

Mitchell, Taiyler Simone 2021, "Children are not supposed to die': CDC director gives passionate response about how children make up 400 of the 600,000 COVID-19 deaths', *Insider*, 26 July 2021, <https://www.insider.com/children-are-not-supposed-die-children-us-died-covid-19-2021-7>.

Zielinski, Alex 2016, 'CPS Ignored Thousands of Texas Foster Kids At Risk of Abuse', *San Antonio Current*, 5 October 2016, <https://www.sacurrent.com/sanantonio/cps-ignored-thousands-of-texas-foster-kids-at-risk-of-abuse/Content?oid=2555523>.

Sanchez, Melissa and Duaa Eldeib 2021, 'Illinois' Child Welfare Agency Continues to Fail Spanish-Speaking Families', *ProPublica*, 31 August 2021, <https://www.propublica.org/ article/illinois-child-welfare-agency-continues-to-fail-spanish-speaking-families>.

Sanchez, Melissa and Duaa Eldeib 2019, 'You're Destroying Families', *ProPublica*, 20 June 2019, <https://features.propublica.org/illinois-dcfs/illinois-child-welfare-agency-burgos-consent-decree-spanish-language-issues/>.

Gunderson, Erica 2021, 'ProPublica: DCFS Not Providing Services for Spanish Speakers', *WTTW News*, 18 September 2021, <https://news.wttw.com/2021/09/18/propublica-dcfs-not-providing-services-spanish-speakers>.

Chapter Fifteen

WDAM Staff and Mia Monet 2022, 'Man accused of shooting at, threatening CPS worker in Jones Co.', *WDAM*, 6 May 2022, <https://www.wdam.com/2022/05/06/cps-worker-shot-threatened-jones-county/>.

Acronyms

ACLU	American Civil Liberties Union
CASA	National CASA/GAL Association for Children and Court Appointed Special Advocate
CPS	Child Protective Services
DACA	Deferred Action for Childhood Arrivals
DCFS	Department of Children and Family Services
DFPS	U.S. Department of Family and Protective Services
DHS	U.S. Department of Homeland Security
DOJ	U.S. Department of Justice
FCA	Fostering Connections Act of 2008
GAL	Guardian Ad Litem
HHS	U.S. Department of Health and Human Services
ICE	U.S. Immigration and Customs Enforcement
IMSS	Instituto Mexicano del Seguro Social (Mexican Institute of Social Security)
ISSSTE	Instituto de Seguridad y Servicios Sociales de Trabajadores (Mexican Civil Service Social Security and Services Institute)
OIG	U.S. Office of Inspector General

ORR	U.S. Office of Refugee Resettlement
PMC	Permanent Managing Conservatorship
SSA	Secretaría de Salud (Mexican Federal Secretary of Health)
TPR	Termination of Parental Rights
UAC	Unaccompanied Alien Children
UNAM	Universidad Nacional Autónoma de México (National Autonomous University of Mexico)
VA	Veterans Administration

About the Author

Richard Villasana, founder of Forever Homes for Foster Kids, is a leading international authority on immigration issues and foster families. A proud Navy veteran, Richard has been featured on CNN International, Univision, AP News, ABC TV, Costco Connections, Washington Post, and EFE, the world's largest Spanish language media company.

He is an international speaker and trainer and has translated for the United Nations. Richard was honored as a California Hero. Richard is also the leading advocate for Latino foster children in the U.S. For nearly 30 years, his nonprofit has worked with government agencies across the country to find families for foster and immigrant children to create a permanent home.

For more information, email
media@ForeverHomesforFosterKids.org.

Please share this book with those
you know will resonate with the message
we are sharing.

We invite reviews!

Made in the USA
Las Vegas, NV
19 September 2022